# Reiki Jin Kei Do

## The Way of Compassion and Wisdom

Steve Gooch

BOOKS

Winchester, U.K.
New York, U.S.A.

First published by O Books, 2006
O Books is an imprint of John Hunt Publishing Ltd., The Bothy,
Deershot Lodge, Park Lane, Ropley, Hants, SO24 0BE, UK
office1@o-books.net
www.o-books.net

Distribution in:

UK and Europe
Orca Book Services
orders@orcabookservices.co.uk
Tel: 01202 665432
Fax: 01202 666219 Int. code (44)

Singapore
STP
davidbuckland@tlp.com.sg
Tel: 65 6276
Fax: 65 6276 7119

USA and Canada
NBN
custserv@nbnbooks.com
Tel: 1 800 462 6420
Fax: 1 800 338 4550

South Africa
Alternative Books
altbook@peterhyde.co.za
Tel: 27 011 792 7730
Fax: 27 011 792 7787

Australia
Brumby Books
sales@brumbybooks.com
Tel: 61 3 9761 5535
Fax: 61 3 9761 7095

Text copyright Steve Gooch

Design: Jim Weaver

ISBN-13: 978 1 905047 85 7
ISBN-10: 1 905047 85 1

A CIP catalogue record for this book is available from the British Library.

Printed in the US by Maple Vail

# Dedication

Dedicated to Seiji Takamori for his wisdom,
compassion and inspiration and to my
two beautiful children, Marianne and Sam
— both gifts from God.

# Acknowledgements

There are a number of people to whom I would particularly like to offer my thanks for their help in getting this book finished and keeping me on track when I was about to derail! I especially want to thank my Reiki Masters, Gordon and Dorothy Bell for initiating me into Reiki in the first place, for their shining example of the true meaning of 'Reiki Master' and for their many insightful comments on the script as it evolved over the months, without which this book would be considerably less than it is. I also wish to thank the lineage head, Dr Ranga Premaratna, for his positive support for this project, for his time in answering all of my questions and for the example that he sets to all in the lineage as a true Master of the teachings. Also thanks go to Felix Yap, Judy Cabral and Ian Pordon for their constant encouragement and moral support, and for listening to all of my complaints patiently and with understanding, before giving me the boot that I needed to get me back to the task of getting the book written. To Dave Price for his help with the preparation of the final typescript and for his proofreading skills, and to Tony Birdfield for allowing me access to his MA dissertation on the teachings of *Reiki Jin Kei Do*. Also to many other Masters of the lineage for their encouragement, constant support, offers of help and advice and for the Reiki that was sent to help manifest this project. I offer you all much love and my deeply felt gratitude.

Finally, I want to offer my thanks to my two children Marianne and Sam for just being themselves and bringing so much goodness into my life.

# Contents

# Foreword

In 1990, my teacher, Seiji Takamori entrusted me with his priceless teachings which have come to be known as Reiki Jin Kei Do and *Buddho-EnerSense*. It was his fervent wish that I should not only preserve these teachings but carry on his work of developing them further and to propagate them world-wide. As Seiji and I said our goodbyes, the enormity of the mission that my teacher had given to me and the responsibility that went with it, began to slowly sink in. My journey through life with these wonderful teachings had only just begun and I certainly did not feel at that point in time up to the task that had been laid on my shoulders.

In the years that followed I did not actively promote the teachings of Seiji Takamori in any significant way. However just as Seiji had predicted, students from all over the world began to visit me at my home in Australia to receive training in these two special systems of meditation and healing. Although I have continued to maintain a relatively low profile students still come as word of mouth has spread Seiji's method, philosophy and teachings around the globe. I estimate that as a particular and distinct style of Reiki we now have thousands of students and teachers of Reiki and *Buddho-EnerSense* world-wide.

Seiji predicted that Reiki Jin Kei Do would play a major role in the healing of the planet's woes. With this in mind and due to world events that continue to have disastrous consequences for the human race such as the many wars that afflict us and the terrible consequences of huge natural disasters, I believe that the time has now arrived for Reiki Jin Kei Do to step into the limelight as a major Reiki lineage. In doing so we are inviting the world-wide Reiki community and all seekers after the truth of personal liberation from suffering to join us – our Reiki Jin Kei Do family – on this incredible journey through Seiji's teachings.

It is the healing of the mind that is at the heart of the Reiki Jin Kei Do teachings and not just the improvement and strengthening of our physical health. It is an emphasis in Reiki that is somewhat different to the approaches of other traditions. Whatever our orientation to the system of Reiki, the important thing is to test the substance and ability to transform lives of the teachings themselves, and this is the real measure of any spiritual or healing method.

I believe that Reiki Jin Kei Do offers a clear and logical explanation of Reiki as a path of healing and spiritual development. If the benefit of the teachings is realized then the individual should follow the teachings and make them their way of life. If not then it is necessary to find the method that is of benefit. It is the teachings and the impact that they have on our lives that are the most important.

I was delighted to hear about Steve Gooch's writing of a book on our lineage of Reiki. He has done an admirable job in researching the roots of Reiki Jin Kei Do and in providing the world with a window on this particular system of meditation and healing. The teachings of Reiki Jin Kei Do as revealed in this book provide new insights into the system of Reiki as it evolved in Japan but with its roots in the spiritual traditions of India, Tibet and Nepal.

As a consequence of his efforts Steve has become a spokesperson for the Reiki Jin Kei Do lineage, which includes all of its past as well as present teachers. I am grateful to Steve for undertaking the task of presenting to the public the teachings and experiences that taking the Reiki Jin Kei Do 'path' can lead to. It is a path that I, he and many others have taken to not only enhance our own lives but also the lives of many others.

I know that this book will be of great benefit to all Reiki Jin Kei Do practitioners, the wider global Reiki community and to the general public.

Dr Ranga J Premaratna (PhD)
Sydney, Australia.
September 2005.

# Introduction

You never enjoy the world aright, till the sea itself
floweth in your veins, till you are clothed with the
heavens and crowned with the stars.

*Thomas Traherne*

When I first came to Reiki back in 1995 I didn't realize then
what a profound teaching I was to be given by my Reiki Masters,
Gordon and Dorothy Bell. It was at a time in my life when things
really couldn't have gotten much worse. You may have seen those
charts that statistically inclined psychologists produce where they
list all of the factors and life events that are most likely to lead to
severe stress or depression. I had the top five altogether in the
space of a two-year period. Life was no fun at all. I had always
been quite a spiritual person but it was hard to stay positive, or
summon up any belief that life could in any way get better for me.
Then I discovered Reiki, and it changed everything. From a life
without hope or purpose I found not only hope and purpose, but
in Reiki a constant, loving, forgiving and non-judging companion.

Things have not always worked out how I would like in my life since then of course, but never again will I find myself at the bottom of a deep dark hole without hope. Reiki is with me all of the time, and for that I live in eternal gratitude to not only my Reiki Masters, Gordon and Dorothy, but also to the spirit of divine love that held my hand and guided me to them.

If you're an old hand at Reiki you won't be surprised to hear that since that time miracles have become a normal part of my life. Little miracles, big miracles, life-changing miracles and miracles that just make you smile. Reiki is always there, gently and humbly bringing life back into balance for those that it touches. What often struck me, however, was the profoundness of these miracles, not just for me, but for others too, particularly for some of my students to whom I eventually went on to teach Reiki. This wasn't just healing in the medical sense, or even just healing in the sense that the energy aware holistic therapy junkies would know it, but a deep and profound healing of the spirit that went beyond anything I had ever experienced up to that time.

At the heart of the teachings that I received from Gordon and Dorothy is a practice not of hands-on healing, but of self-discovery. With the exception of a handful of independent Reiki teachers it is a practice, an orientation, of Reiki that is now only just starting to emerge within other traditions of Reiki. This is as consequence of the efforts of some prominent figures within the Reiki community undertaking their own research into the origins of the system. Yet, so often today Reiki is used in a limited way (yet immensely meaningful on the level of mundane reality). We read all the time in Reiki book after Reiki book about some newly discovered 'original' method of using Reiki as a healing therapy, yet all of these methods miss the point to a degree – healing is so much more than simply fixing a bad back or doing away with arthritis – and however complex or clever the method is, they do not even begin to hint at the full potential of the system that was originally left to us. I don't belittle this profoundly special and indescribably beautiful healing that so many people are experiencing, but there is so much more beyond this! Reiki – the method – can open the door to the infinite, indeed, it not only can, but does so every time that it is invoked, but how many of us are aware that the door is even there, let alone that it has been opened for us? All we have to do is re-orientate ourselves to the divine spark within us and follow the light – that is the beauty of Reiki – it is a tool to show us the way to our own experience of oneness with the All. Of course, Reiki – the 'energy' – is the All. It is an opportunity. It is an opportunity for each one of us to grow and discover ourselves, and then find that there was never anything really to discover, just the bliss of oneness. As TS Eliot once noted:

> We must not cease from exploration and the end of all our exploring will be to arrive where we began and to know the place for the first time.

This is the gift that Reiki offers us, to know ourselves for the first time and thus to enable others, through a deep and profound healing to know themselves for the first time also.

So often I come across advertisements for beauty treatment salons that will give you a bit of a makeover and throw in a quick reflexology treatment and some Reiki, as if it was no more than a special kind of lipstick. Of course, most Reiki practitioners have a little more understanding of the healing and therapeutic potential of their abilities than that, but how many of them are using the method in the way that it was really intended? How many of them realize that there is more to Reiki than its potential to heal? Reiki is not just a complementary therapy. Fortunately, as our knowledge of Reiki's true origins grows, more and more people are becoming aware of the possibilities for deeply engaging with the system and thus exploiting its true potential as a deep and profound method of healing on all levels.

The vessel that is Reiki Jin Kei Do (The Way of Compassion and Wisdom Through Reiki) contains an original method of

Reiki, it is a method that strikes at the heart of the Usui system. This is not to suggest that Reiki Jin Kei Do is *the* original method or that it contains the whole truth of Reiki in its original form. It is a method of Reiki however that is redolent of the system that Usui first developed and has an orientation to practice that is believed to be in many senses very much like Usui's own early approach and understanding. It is not a re-constructed system, and contains no New Age teachings or methods, nothing that is channelled and is entirely without input from the newly emerging material on Reiki from Japan. It is very much a work-in-progress however, and has developed since it was first disseminated in the West. A number of methods for engaging with the system have been incorporated to provide students with extra tools that befit the philosophy and aims of the lineage. It also contains an acknowledgment of its common ancestry with Western Reiki through its teaching of Reiki Therapeutics, that is, Reiki as a hands-on therapy. This is not regarded as a focus of the system, but simply another way of expressing the true heart of Reiki — that of self-knowledge through the expression of compassion for all beings.

Reiki Jin Kei Do (RJKD) is the name given to the lineage, (the frame), which contains a method of practice that although distinctly Buddhist in feel, is, like all Reiki methods, available to all, and transcends narrow boundaries of religiosity or philosophy. I have taught this system of Reiki to people of many faiths in the UK and in Egypt, and found that, with the exception of those few who hold rather extreme views in relation to their religious calling, all find the teachings easily accessible and immensely rewarding through adding another dimension to their lives and thus a deeper commitment to their own core spiritual values.

In this book I intend to explore the philosophy behind Reiki — the teachings of RJKD. You will not find any of the specific methods or techniques of the lineage described in here, nor will you see the Reiki symbols. Gordon and Dorothy have asked me not to reveal this material, and that is enough. A part of honoring

my teachers is also to honor their teachings. What you will find
is an exploration of Reiki that is new, at least in printed form. A
re-orientation if you will. A way of looking at the system that will
take you beyond Reiki as a complementary therapy (or as a form
of lipstick!) and hopefully lead you to a better understanding of
how you can approach your own healing into oneness, and bring
you closer to the divine spark that is inherent within you, and
ultimately to merge with it, because it is you.

RJKD also contains the teachings of the older Buddhist system
of which Reiki is a simplified form. This is now known as *Buddho-
EnerSense*. This spiritual method parallels many fundamentals of
the widely known Reiki system, including information relating
to the Reiki symbols. *Buddho-EnerSense* is taught in four levels,
and deals in depth with the historical origins of many aspects of
the Reiki system and provides a profound set of teachings and
disciplines that allows the student to more fully explore their own
spiritual development within the framework of the system, though
as with Reiki, there is no need for the student to subscribe to
Buddhism as a belief to fully engage with the material of *Buddho-
EnerSense*. *Buddho-EnerSense* however will not be covered within the
pages of this book. The system, in all of its complexity and depth,
would require a book of its own, and as such this is a project for
another time. I have therefore restricted this present work to an
exploration of Reiki within RJKD though it has been at times
necessary to draw on material from the *Buddho-EnerSense* system.

I make no claims for the Reiki energy of RJKD being better or
more powerful than anyone else's Reiki. Reiki is Reiki, regardless
of who is channelling it. It is all the same. I state this clearly as from
time to time various Reiki Masters use the 'my Reiki is better than
your Reiki' strategy as a selling point. This is a product of the ego.
Whether or not the experience of Reiki from this lineage is more
powerful for a student or client than from someone from another
lineage is entirely subjective. Everyone is different, and will feel the
energies differently. Approach Reiki with an open and loving heart
and it will work miracles for you – there is no order in miracles.

I have tried to approach the material from as 'universalist' a standpoint as I can. Although much of the material is in part or wholly derived from the Buddhist canon, I do not have the intention of addressing only Buddhists. This book has been written for all. I hope that there is material in here that will whet the appetite of those who are new to Reiki, and also provide some food for thought for those familiar with the system already. For those of you who have already trained within this lineage, my hope is that this book will help to guide your practice and understanding of the teachings that you have.

Much material, particularly the wisdom of the lineage head and my Reiki Masters, has been drawn upon in the writing of this work, and so many of you that have already trained in RJKD will find familiar stories and analogies from your own Reiki training in this lineage, but the book is in essence my personal orientation on the teachings and methods. I make no claim to be an expert on these teachings, and am still very much engaged in my own journey through them. I hope however that what is presented here does give a snapshot of the sublime and deeply profound teachings that are at the heart of Reiki Jin Kei Do.

As word spread throughout the lineage that I was writing a book on our teachings, I began to receive large numbers of e-mails from all over the world. Without fail, the Masters that contacted me offered many words of encouragement, huge amounts of enthusiasm and more help than I could ever have hoped for. There was clearly a deep sense that it was time for someone to bring the teachings, methods and philosophy of this lineage to a wider public as it had spent long enough in the hinterlands of the Reiki community. I hope therefore that I have done justice to the lineage and have strengthened in some ways the bond of connectivity and sense of family that we all feel within Reiki Jin Kei Do. But this book is mainly for those who are new to Reiki or are looking for a different approach to the system. I hope that you may find what you are looking for within these pages.

# 1

# What is Reiki?

*What a man takes in by contemplation, that he pours out in love.*

*Meister Eckhart*

When I am asked this question by people who have never heard of Reiki before, I tend to give one of three stock answers that will give a sufficient anchor for them to be able to pigeon hole it into some sort of category. This sets up a frame of reference for them and allows me to expand on the subject if necessary. In a nutshell, these answers are:

1. A form of energy.
2. A form of hands-on healing – a complementary therapy.
3. A system of personal spiritual development.

So these are our frames of reference, and the basis on which I intend to explore the subject of Reiki and take you further into an understanding of what this energetic discipline actually is.

Many people reading this book will already be familiar with Reiki to some extent or another and will have their own internal working definition of it. Perhaps you have read one or two books on the subject or surfed the net and discovered that Reiki is one of the family of energetic healing disciplines along with crystal healing and aromatherapy, amongst others. The chances are that your understanding of Reiki then will come under definition number 2 above. This is fine as a starting point, but Reiki is much, much more than this and from the standpoint of the teachings of this particular tradition of Reiki, this is not the most significant of the three ways of approaching and understanding the subject. Far more significant and profound are the other two definitions; numbers 1 and 3. This is not to marginalize or to dismiss the notion of Reiki as a healing therapy, but it needs to be seen in a much wider context. Ultimately Reiki cannot be defined by any one of the three definitions above, it is the sum total of all of them, and in fact much more besides. Without an acceptance of this no real understanding is possible and thus, whether you are an old hand at Reiki or a relative newcomer, you will fail to gain the maximum benefit in your life that the discipline has to offer.

I suppose that the one problem with trying to fully understand Reiki is that its depths are as infinite as the universe itself. It is way beyond the scope of this book to even begin to cover the subject in that much detail – a lifetime of study and practice is needed. What we can do is begin to look at some of the basic descriptors and potentialities of what Reiki is and has to offer. This will provide a working knowledge of the system that will allow us to explore it more fully in our own daily lives and so develop a much more profound and intimate understanding of it. The best place to start in unwrapping Reiki is with the word itself. What does it actually mean?

## Reiki – The Word

The word 'Reiki' is Japanese, and in Japan it is not used in the way that it has come to be used in the West. This is principally due to the problems of accurate translation from Japanese into

English. In Japanese, the word 'Reiki' would not fit two of our descriptors above as it does not describe any sort of system, whether of hands-on healing or of spiritual development. There is however, a definition that is pretty much universally accepted. 'Reiki' is formed from two distinct Japanese characters (*kanji*); '*Rei*' and '*Ki*'.

*Rei* — Spirit/Spiritual/Universal

*Ki* — Energy

The combined meaning of the two characters '*Rei-Ki*' therefore is 'Spiritual Energy', or a higher form of energy. It is often referred to in the West as 'Universal Life Force Energy' or simply 'Universal Energy', but this misses the point to some degree. We need to put more of an emphasis on the fact that the word is referring to SPIRITUAL energy. Other ways of describing 'spirit' or 'spiritual' might be as 'consciousness', or 'life principle' or 'mind'. When we talk about Consciousness or Pure Consciousness we are referring to that which is the common medium of which we are all a part — the limitless Universal Energy Field or Universal Mind.

## The Universal Energy Field

The Universal Energy Field is formless, yet all form is created from it. It is literally everywhere and everything. It is omnipresent, omniscient and omnipotent. It has no beginning and it has no end. The Universal Energy Field is our essential spiritual nature. It is the state of Pure Bliss or Unconditional Love, out of which everything manifests, including us. It is often referred to as Buddha Nature or God/Cosmic Consciousness. It is that which maintains and promotes all life and is of a much higher vibrational frequency than the physical world that is all around us. Yet the two are the same. Imagine for a moment that the Universal Energy Field is a vast expanse of water and we, along with all other physical things, are chunks of ice floating in it. We are still of the same stuff as the surrounding ocean of energy, but we no longer recognize our commonality with it and think of ourselves as separate individuals. Just as ice is a solidified or condensed form of water, we are solidified forms of universal, spiritual energy. In essence, both are identical. Our connectedness with this blissful state of energetic existence and each and every other being in the universe was illustrated in a study that was reported by Rupert Sheldrake when he noted that rats taught a particular task in, say, the UK, would through their connection to what he termed a '*morphogenetic field*', enable rats in Australia to learn the same task a lot more quickly. This study has been replicated many times over.

Vivekananda describes our state of interconnectedness and interdependence in this way:

> In an ocean there are huge waves, then smaller waves, and still smaller, down to little bubbles; but back of all these is the infinite ocean. The bubble is connected with the infinite ocean at one end, and the huge wave at the other end. So one may be a gigantic man, and another a little bubble; but each is connected with that infinite ocean of energy which is the common birthright of every animal that exists. Wherever there is life, the store house of infinite energy is behind it.

The essence and power of this concept was very beautifully described by Mrs Hawayo Takata – the woman who originally brought Reiki to the West:

I believe that there exists One Supreme Being – the Absolute Infinite – a dynamic force that governs the world and universe. It is an unseen spiritual power that vibrates and all other powers fade into insignificance beside it...This power is unfathomable, immeasurable, and being a universal life force, it is incomprehensible to man. Yet every single living being is receiving its blessings daily, awake or asleep...

So how are we energetically connected to Vivekananda's 'infinite ocean of energy' so that we may receive these blessings? If we look at the concepts described in Buddhist yogic philosophy we see that the human being is considered to be made up of several layers of energy of different densities. The first layer, which is dependent upon the individual's *karma*, is the manifestation of the person's consciousness into physicality, the physical body. The second layer is generally referred to as the *etheric* or *pranic* body. This fine energy field, which is of a higher vibration, surrounds and envelops the physical body. The next layer, which is of an extremely high vibrational frequency, is called the *mental* body and this is where our thoughts and emotions arise and then pass away in a constant flow. The fourth layer, our *spiritual* body, is the one that connects all the other bodies to the Universal Energy Field and is again of a higher vibrational frequency than those preceding it. The Universal Energy Field or *universal* body penetrates all of the other energy bodies, including the dense physical body.

Today, through supergravitation theory, quantum physics is starting to recognize the existence of the Universal Energy Field; a perfectly balanced and standardized field of pure energy that stands only in relationship to itself. Scientists are beginning to acknowledge that there is an intrinsic and fundamental link between our minds and the material universe and that thought affects this great energy field. It is regarded as a field of pure intelligence (mind), a gigantic thought, and that this thought, or consciousness has a particular kind of creative inter-relationship with itself, the 'friction' of which, in slowing down time, creates the circumstances from which matter is manifested to form the basis of creation. This concept seems set to overthrow the philosophy of materialism. There is a dawning realization that existence is in fact a network of relationships, and that relationship underlies everything – the relationship of the part to the whole – and that each part, even elementary sub-atomic particles, might possess a basic level of consciousness.

This theory is an aspect of Western cosmology that is dependent on the notion of the Big Bang – the birth of the universe in which the primordial unity which existed before the formation of the stars and planets was rent asunder to form two polar opposites that set in motion the ceaseless flux of creation. This concept was first laid down in the *Tao Teh Ching* many centuries ago, when it said "One gave birth to two" (the two being *yin* and *yang*). The polarity to which they gave rise and the consequent birth of everything in the universe is known as *The Great Principle of Yin and Yang. Yang*, being the more rarefied and immaterial was considered as the Universal Energy Field – heaven, while *yin* was more condensed and physical, and sank down to become earth. The ceaseless interplay of these two complementary forces through formation, dissolution, interaction and transmutation are what constitutes the primal motive force of our existence.

The theories of Quantum physics rely on the hypothetical existence of eleven different dimensions to explain its highly complex extrapolations of how the universe works (*membrane theory*). In 1999 James E Bleicher, in his work on the theoretical model of the fifth dimension, stated "The pattern of field variations in the fifth dimension…is the extra something that distinguishes a living organism from a simple Newtonian mechanism." He went on to say "The linked field patterns, couplings or entanglements that are characteristic of living organisms are the life force, vitalistic force or *élan vital* that scholars and philosophers have sought for many centuries." In the same paper, he also had this revealing comment to make:

Mind is thus a still higher level of complexity than life because it represents the control of life…Awareness can only be explained in physics as a point of view or perspective that can only come as the result of perception from a higher dimension of spacetime. Mind is the five-dimensional extension of the complexity of our four-dimensional brains.

We do not observe the fifth dimension directly and can only perceive the higher…dimension through such non-material qualities and quantities as memory, thought, feelings and other paraphysical concepts.

Further interesting work from a different scientific perspective is being done at Princeton University through the Global Consciousness Project.

When we talk of *ki* we are referring to the energy once it has manifested in the physical realm. It is the body's vital energy and that of all living things and is an aspect of *Rei* that is modified so that it becomes compatible with the different life forms within this material existence. Yet it is still the *stuff* of the Universal Energy Field. It is the basic building block of all matter. It is that which animates all living things and is as Daniel Reid noted in *Chi Gung – Harnessing the Power of the Universe*:

> …the fundamental functional force that drives all activities and transformations in nature and the universe, from the galactic to the microscopic, from the birth, growth, decay and death of stars to the formation and dissolution of atoms, molecules and cells in the human body.

Depending on the accessing tools – the ability of the practitioner, this energy has the potential to manifest many different frequencies. In fact, as it passes through the body and the various organs its frequency will change depending on the needs and functions of the organs. However it cannot be measured by known scientific instruments, but we can have the experience of it effecting physical reality. We could draw an analogy between this sea of universal energy and something like electricity.

When we switch on a light bulb for instance or turn on the radio or an electric heater we are using a particular type of tool to transform electricity into light, sound or heat. Electricity is simply the flow of electrons. The accessing tool that we use converts this undifferentiated energy into a form that can be detected by us through the use of our physical senses. When we (the accessing tool) channel *ki*, we do so by changing its form so that it is compatible with our physical nature as it comes from the infinite energy source. As we refer to the energy source as *Rei* we thus call this manifested energy *Reiki* to denote its origins within the Universal Energy Field.

The *ki* that we are referring to here is the same energy that underpins the practice of many traditional healing methods such as Chinese acupuncture, or reflexology. In Chinese it is known as *chi*, the Hindus refer to it as *prana* and the Kahunas as *mana*. It is also known as *bioplasmic energy* by Russian researchers, *orgon* by Dr Wilhelm Reich and *odic power* by Baron Reichenbach. Pythagoras called it *pneuma* and Paracelsus referred to it as *archaeus*. There are many other names for this energy, and it has been identified as the energetic basis of all life across all cultures over the centuries, and is recognized as that which controls the vital functions of the human system and that it is the principle factor responsible for the state of human health and disease. It is the fundamental gauge of our vitality and longevity and the bridge that connects body and mind, being the common factor in the complex equations of our physical, emotional and spiritual life.

## Searching for Yourself

Ultimately Reiki, the system, is a spiritual growth tool and those that are attracted to Reiki have already begun their journey along the path of self-awareness and are open to the changes that will come into their lives. Reiki is a tool that you can use to open up all areas of your life. You can use it to help you realize your innate creative abilities, and to help you break down any mental blocks that you may have to both giving and receiving the abundance of the universe in what ever form it may ultimately manifest. The physical and mental health that Reiki promotes is an added benefit that occurs as the energy melts away the blocks in awareness that stifle a true sense of wellbeing.

It is important to make it clear that Reiki is not reliant upon any particular belief system, religion or spiritual concept. Whilst it grew out of aspects of Buddhist practice and philosophy amongst other things, it aligns itself with no particular tradition, whether Buddhist or not and does not require any belief or practice within the methods or belief systems that influenced its development. It is a truly universal and non-judgmental system of spiritual enquiry that is compatible with all beliefs and spiritual concepts or practices.

Within this tradition of Reiki, Reiki Jin Kei Do there exist a number of methods designed to lead the practitioner to a better understanding and realization of their innate connectedness to the Universal Energy Field. This is developed through the expansion of compassion and wisdom within the practitioner for the betterment of all beings.

Through the consistent application of practices such as meditation it is possible to access the field of energy that is our spiritual body. Yogic breathing along with meditation can amplify the energy of the mental body to the higher vibration of the spiritual body. By bringing the scattered and distracted mind to a state of *samadhi* (one-pointed concentration), which is a high-energy state, the practitioner develops an awareness of high-energy states beyond that of the mental body. As our consciousness learns to recognize these high-energy states we are in the realm of the spiritual body, which is close in frequency to that of the universal body, or Universal Consciousness or Universal Energy Field.

In using Reiki as a spiritual practice for our own development we are ultimately able to connect to and access the vibrations of the spiritual body. With further practice and training and the deepening of our *samadhi* or *dhyanic state* (losing the sense of being in meditation and simply being aware of one's existence) we can reach the point of experiencing the universal pure state of consciousness. We find that the freedom for which we had been searching was ours all along, and that there is no reason to continue with our search for some 'true self'. We find that we always were our true self, because it is not possible to be anything other, and all we need to do is to allow our identification with the body/mind to pass through, and just 'be' who and what we are. It is not an easy road to travel, embedded in the material world of suffering and temporary relief from suffering as we are, but as Stephen Covey noted in *The 7 Habits of Highly Effective People*, you simply have to travel the road. There are no shortcuts, there are no other roads, and we cannot get to where we are going without going the way that we are. We cannot simply parachute into the terrain and proclaim enlightenment or oneness with God. What is important is how we orientate ourselves to this journey. As Jack Kornfield has said "In undertaking a spiritual life, what matters is simple: We must make certain that our path is connected with our heart." It takes commitment and dedication from a center of love.

In this spirit of love we should be gentle with ourselves. It can become very easy to commit to our discipline and simply engage in a form of spiritual self-flagellation, almost as if we were punishing ourselves for something or for not making enough progress as fast as we would like. It is easy to slip into this, particularly when life is not going in the direction that we want, and so Reiki becomes a drudge and a moral obligation as we try to force a state of being into existence for ourselves that we are not ready for or is not appropriate for us at that particular time.

Reiki will have a profound impact on your life if you allow it to guide you. The more that you are willing to learn and grow with Reiki the more it will work through you, and the deeper the changes will be. The only limits to this change are those that are put there by your own conscious and unconscious beliefs. There is a plan for all of us, which is not based on what others or society think is right for us. They do not know. Neither is it dependent on our social or cultural background. We need to tune into our own inner promptings and work to live by them. Use your intuition and judgment to guide you, and be open to what life presents you with. The more that you trust in Reiki, the more it will guide your steps without fault. A beautiful saying in Reiki is: *'Let go and let Reiki'*.

## Reiki as Hands-on Healing

Throughout human history, healing methods have existed that involved the transfer of energy from or through one person to another. Everyone has the innate ability to transfer Universal Energy, either directly from source or from their own reserves of this energy in much the same way, at least as is externally apparent, as is done with Reiki and it is the healing potential of Reiki that is most widely known in the West. There are however some important differences between Reiki and other forms of spiritual healing. The most obvious of these is that Reiki is one of the few systems of spiritual healing where a person's natural ability to channel energy is enhanced through an *'attunement'* process (discussed later). This gives a quick, certain and permanent connection to Universal Energy. In other forms of spiritual healing the ability has to be worked at, refined and developed over a number of months or even years. Of course there is also the problem that many non-Reiki healers often give to some degree or another of their own energy. The pure connection to the universe is not always present. They may well be channelling from the universe but there is a good chance that they are also channelling from themselves. This leaves the person channelling the healing energy either physically or mentally exhausted at the end of a treatment session. In Reiki this is never the case. In fact a Reiki practitioner can often feel more energized at the end of a healing session than they did at the beginning, as the energy passes through the body of the practitioner.

Healing is done by channelling Reiki energy, from the Universal Energy Field through the body (specifically through the Crown, Third Eye, Throat and Heart *chakras*), out of the hands and into the recipient. Reiki is probably the simplest and one of the most natural methods of healing. It is also the most effective way of transferring Universal Energy. Because the practitioner's own energy is not used it is also useful as a self-healing method. As a consequence of the attunement process a person is opened up to become a channel through which the Universal Energy can of its own accord manifest its potential in concentrated form via the hands of the practitioner in the form of healing.

In the healing system of Reiki we need to be aware that we do not 'give' people Reiki. We can be a channel, through which this energy can manifest, but it is the recipient of the energy that is drawing it through us, and in the process we also receive a healing experience. In Reiki classes, I describe this process to my students as being a bit like a tap connected to a reservoir via a length of pipe, where the Reiki channel is the length of pipe. The pipe does not control how much water will end up in the bucket, but it makes it possible for the person turning the tap to get as much as they require from the limitless reservoir. In the process of drawing the water, the inside of the pipe also gets wet, although this was not the reason why the tap was originally turned on. Because of this process of drawing the energy it is never possible to give someone too much Reiki. All we need to do is provide the optimum circumstances for the recipient to take their own healing journey, by being the best pipe that we can!

But what goes on in a Reiki treatment? The following quote from *Teach Yourself Reiki* by Sandi Leir Shuffrey gives a good indication:

> By treating someone else we are, in effect, assisting in the reclamation of their personal power. Reiki practice is like an offering, an extension of the vital energetic spirit, that is drawn through the hands. Healing occurs as an interaction between

the energy body of the receiver and the unlimited external Life Force drawn in via the practitioner. The energy field reacts instantly to any changes in feeling, thought or chemistry, expanding through relaxation that which has contracted through stress and tension.

Reiki works then on the material, etheric and subtle levels and thus relieves physical and emotional pain and promotes spiritual clarity by restoring and balancing the natural life force energy within the physical and energetic bodies. The word 'healing' is derived from the Anglo-Saxon word *healan*, which refers not only to the healing of the physical body, but the spiritual body as well and this is precisely what Reiki does. In working on the spiritual level it can aid in bringing lucidity to one's function and mission in life, and thus profound healing can take place at this level, regardless of the state of the physical body. Indeed the recipient does not need to be ill or in any kind of discomfort at all to receive Reiki as it can also be used for disease prevention and health maintenance.

A series of light hand positions are used over the fully clothed body that cover the recipients' *chakras* and *nadis*. Specific hand positions may be laid down within the treatment protocol of the practitioner, or can involve a more intuitive approach. RJKD teaches both approaches.

It is important to recognize that the person 'doing' Reiki is not a healer. To claim this title is to claim mastery of the Reiki energy, and to assume that somehow it is possible to dictate what will happen in the healing process. This is not the case. To try to do so will simply block the flow of energy and interfere with the healing process. We can be a channel for the energy, and we can bring it to bear on different parts of the body, but ultimately it is Reiki that is the healer, and it will do whatever work is necessary for the highest good of the recipient, and this may not always be what we or the recipient might want. It is important to remember that Reiki is pure intelligence, the stuff of life, and it knows better than our limited conscious minds what is right for any particular individual. If you simply allow Reiki to do its work, it will ultimately open your mind to an understanding of how the body functions and is created and what sustains and what destroys it prematurely. With this knowledge, all healing is possible.

Because of the inherent spiritual basis of the Reiki system – even when used simply as a healing therapy – this can, as Barbara Emerson made clear in her book *Self-Healing Reiki* lead to its non-acceptance by the medical community. Reiki can be seen as some sort of pseudo-religious New Age flakiness that is best held at arm's length. This is a problem for those who seriously want to undertake work as a practitioner of Reiki Therapeutics. However, I do not believe that it is appropriate to try to hide Reiki's fundamental underpinnings as a spiritual growth tool, or try to change the system in some way to make it fit a model who's delimited features are so much less, and so much more restrictive in terms of its capabilities and potentialities to heal than the full spectrum of deeply engaged Reiki methods and practices. It should not be necessary for Reiki to hide its true colors, but for the medical profession to accept Reiki for what it is. This said, many people are managing to find work as hands-on therapists in various settings, and the trend for Reiki's acceptance into the realm of 'conventional' medical practices is continuing to grow dramatically, particularly where it is being used in conjunction with other complementary therapies such as aromatherapy, reflexology and acupuncture.

✳

So these are our definitions of what Reiki is and RJKD draws on all of them to define itself and this bountiful energy that we engage with. RJKD also draws extensively on, and views the energy system through a Buddhist lens to a degree. This is not to marginalize or dismiss other ways of approaching the material. The concepts in RJKD are common to all spiritual paths. The big question is, however, 'how does one go about channelling the energy? How do you 'do' Reiki?

# 2

# The Attunement Process

The moment you have in your heart this extraordinary
thing called love and feel the depth, the delight, the
ecstasy of it, you will discover that for you the world is
transformed.

*J. Krishnamurti*

Fundamental to the practice of Reiki is the process known as an
'attunement' or 'empowerment'. We do need to be clear about
what we mean by these terms however. 'Attunement' generally
refers to the activation and stimulation of the students' own
energy system. 'Empowerment' is a term used for that part of the
Masters level attunement that gives the authority to transmit the
teachings to others. Whatever we call them, these initiations open
you to receiving and channelling Universal Life Force Energy
and re-connect you through lifting the veils of ignorance to that
which is all there is – your universal and infinite birthright as a
spark of light within the mind of God. It is the Reiki attunement,
which can only be performed by a Reiki Master that gives the

student the ability to 'do' Reiki. This does not imply that the Master has control over his or her students, however. The Master is simply someone who can facilitate the opening of the student to the abundant nature of the universe, and has made a life-long commitment to live and grow with Reiki themselves.

It is not possible to simply read a book on Reiki, or for that matter a set of instructions on a website, practice some techniques and thus be able to channel Reiki. We need the attunement from a properly qualified and experienced Reiki Master to gain a pure and permanent connection to the Universal Energy Field. It is normal and preferable to attend a class and be attuned by a Reiki Master in person. Some have claimed that it is possible to perform an attunement over a distance and indeed purport do so as a regular part of their teaching programme. There are many questions over whether it is indeed possible to conduct a Reiki attunement over a distance. However, I personally feel that the Reiki Master owes an obligation of honor in being with a student in person for this profoundly sacred and divinely guided ceremony and that it is also necessary and a point of professional care for the Master to make themselves available should the need arise due to the possibility of powerful physical or emotional blockages being released during or immediately after the process. The student may need some support through this.

In the fields of spiritual development and hands-on healing, it would be a brave or foolish person who would make a guarantee of any kind, but in the case of Reiki, there is at least one guarantee that can be made with confidence, and that is that the attunement process, when done in person, will always work in every case. As long as the initiating Master has received their training to the requisite level and performs the attunement process correctly and with an open and honest heart, it cannot fail. Everyone can be attuned to Reiki whether they believe in it or not. A student's attendance at a Reiki class indicates willingness for the attunement energy to manifest results within them, and this is important, but I have had people attend a class in support of a partner in spite of their own lack of belief or interest, and have found the whole experience quite dull until the attunement process. They changed their outlook entirely when they found that they could feel the Reiki energy manifesting in their hands. Why should this be so? I believe that what the conscious mind thinks or believes plays only a small part in the process. Even though an individual consciousness may not believe in Reiki, it does not alter the fact that the individual's subconscious is fully aware of its connection to and commonality with the Universal Energy Field. Also as Lawrence Ellyard in his book *Reiki Healer* has made clear, the attunement energy, whilst utilizing the body's energy system, is ultimately independent of this system and of the interference of the mind and thus the ego. The ego, as it manifests through emotions and feelings, would otherwise be able to disrupt, block or manipulate this flow of vital energy and the results, in the latter case could potentially be catastrophic or at least unpleasant.

Some Reiki Masters have begun to change elements of the attunement process or to add new practices to it. This is a shame and certainly leads one to suspect the interference of the ego at work in this. There is no need whatsoever to change or modify the attunement process – it works fine just the way it is. Of course it has been argued that once the attunement process has been tampered with in some way then it is not entirely possible to be certain of the outcome or indeed what exactly it is that we are attuning a student to. If we simply use the correct alignment following the traditional methods passed down from one Master to the next then we can be sure that we are supporting the system that we know works and that the results will have a lasting effect. There are variations in the way that traditional attunements are performed, but this is the result of a natural and progressive evolution that inevitably takes on board the particular characteristics of the Reiki Master as well as the lineage from which he or she teaches. This is entirely different from the conscious decision to change or manipulate the system for whatever spurious reasons.

So what exactly goes on in an attunement process or ceremony? I am not going to describe the specifics of this – this is sacred knowledge – held within this lineage at least only by those properly qualified to have access to it. Fundamentally, however, the process involves the student being seated in front of the Reiki Master whilst he or she, through the powerful channelling of Universal Energy, allows the student's physical and energetic bodies to receive and be able to transmit Universal Energy in concentrated form. This process involves the intense focus of the initiating Master on the transmission of energy from the Universal Energy Field, via a channel created within their own energy field, to the student, to increase the energetic 'spin' of various energy centers within the body – the *chakras*, which we shall look at in more detail later. It is worth considering why it is that we talk of increasing the spin of the *chakras*. Energy never moves in straight lines, to increase the energetic quality of anything, we increase its spin-rate. Richard Gordon, in his book *Quantum Touch* noted that:

> From electrons to planets to entire galaxies, everything is in motion, spinning. In terms of mundane physics, a spiralling football or spinning Frisbee cuts through the air more efficiently due to its rotation. Bullets spiral out of a gun, and their spinning motion helps them to go straight with better penetration. When you get the energy spinning, you are raising both the vibration and the potential for the energy to penetrate.

The attunement process involves the drawing of Reiki symbols, the repetition of mantras, breathing exercises and/or blowing of energy to the student along with the conscious intent of the Reiki Master to bring his/her own consciousness into a state of resonance with the vibration of the Universal Energy Field. Through the use of these devices the Master brings his or her mind into sharp focus and this brings their own energy field up to the same vibrational frequency of the Universal Energy Field, thus forming the channel through which the student can draw the energy that they need. If the Master can also still his or her mind through the entering of deep absorptive states then the interference of the ego and of extraneous thoughts is also reduced and so the energy flow is maximized. As already made clear, different Masters and lineages have different approaches. Once complete, the attunement, having left a permanent energetic imprint, allows for the unhindered flow of Universal Energy through the Crown, Third Eye, Throat and Heart *chakras* of the student and then out via energy channels to the palms whenever the student thinks of the energy.

Some people think that the ability to channel Reiki is a special talent or a rare gift from God or the Universe, or based on a powerful belief that it will work. None of these things are true. Belief has no part in any aspect of Reiki, and although it most certainly is a gift from God, it is not a discriminatory gift; only picking out those special people who are worthy. It is a gift to everyone, there is no exclusion. If this were not the case then there would be those who simply could not be attuned to Reiki. I'll say it again: everyone can be attuned to Reiki.

A person who has experienced the sacred technology of a Reiki attunement has undergone a process for fine-tuning the physical and *etheric* bodies to a higher vibratory frequency. This is a bit like tuning in a radio. A radio by its very nature has the potential to broadcast sound from your favorite station but will do nothing until you fine-tune it. The Reiki attunement is our permanent connection to the energy of the universe, as our own energy system, whilst going through this process, receives a memory of a higher state of energy. This memory is locked in to our systems and can be recalled and utilized whenever we need to access that higher energy state. This connection cannot be lost, given away or taken away. It is with us for the rest of our lives.

At 1st Degree the attunements specifically address the physical body by attuning the upper *chakras* and palms. The 2nd Degree attunements work to a much greater extent on the *etheric*, or energy body whilst deepening the ability to channel the Reiki energy, and thus enabling the practitioner to send energy beyond time and space. The Master's attunement magnifies this energetic connection significantly, and addresses all seven of the major *chakras*.

In my classes, in keeping with the way that Gordon and Dorothy taught me, the 1st Degree attunements are split, with the first part of the process being performed on Day 1 of the class and the second on Day 2 of the class. At 2nd Degree the attunements are given as one process on the first day of the class, whilst at Masters Level, due to the length of time required for each individual attunement, students are invited to attend on their own at some convenient time just prior to the start of formal training. There are obviously other formats that can be employed for the giving of attunements, and there is no need to adhere to any particular way, but for most students, this format seems to work fine.

It has been said that the modern way of performing attunements by focusing on the energetic quality of the various *chakras* is a recent development that is not in keeping with the original method of passing on attunements. Historically there is evidence that the original empowerment of Mikao Usui, the discoverer and creator of the Reiki system, was the result of a meditation that directly involved the conscious focus on and empowerment of the *chakras*. This resulted in an experience of mind transformation as the energy manifested in a way that is consistent with well known meditation practices of focusing on the *chakra* system in an attempt to initiate a powerful increase in their vibratory frequency or 'spin'. This subject is looked at further in the next chapter on the history of Reiki. It is the *chakra* system that acts as a series of centers of activity for the reception, assimilation and transmission of life energies. Of course this in no way proves that Usui used the *chakra* system himself in empowering or initiating others, but it does seem to make sense that a process that is designed to increase the energetic connection of the student to the Universal Energy Field would have some sort of bearing or influence on the energetic map of the student's own body. Without addressing the body's energy system there is no way of making a connection to the Universal Energy Field.

There are now many different approaches to performing the Reiki attunements and the method that is employed within RJKD (which is consistent to all Masters within this tradition) is significantly different to the styles and approaches of other lineages and traditions. One of the main differences is that students are not attuned 'conveyor-belt' style – that is lined up in a row, or sat in a circle while the Master either collectively or in increments attunes the group. All students within RJKD are attuned one-to-one at all levels. This is partly in recognition of the fact that the student is making a personal, profound and sacred commitment that is being honored and respected by the individual attention of the initiating Master, but also due to the fact that an individual Reiki attunement process can take anywhere from 20 minutes to a whole hour to perform on each student. For the Masters attunement about 40 minutes to an hour would be the norm, but in practice this could take significantly longer with some students. This is not to imply in any way that simply because the attunements in RJKD are protracted affairs that they are in any way superior or more powerful than the methods employed by others. They are simply our way of approaching the process.

## Effects of The Attunement Process

The Reiki attunements affect everyone differently, and this is dependent on your vibratory frequency when you first receive an attunement. If you have been engaged in practices such as meditation or yoga or in other energy based systems to increase your awareness and thus your own vibratory rate, the attunements will provide a very quick and powerful leap to an even greater opening. For someone that is just beginning a journey of self-enquiry, there is also a powerful leap, but the expansion of energy will be relative to the level that they start with. The real work of an attunement however is done by the recipient through the self-practice of applying Reiki in their own lives on a daily basis and thus maintaining and developing their strong connection to the Universal Energy Field. Our ability to reach higher vibrational states is via our consciousness and thus we need to work on this aspect of ourselves as much as we can. Further attunements at a particular level can augment this energetic development, but are not necessary.

During the attunement process, and also during hands-on treatments, strong visual experiences can occur of a visionary nature. Energy waves can be seen or felt traveling through the body. Lights and colors can be seen. It is important to emphasize that these experiences are of no importance as far as the student's awareness is concerned. For some who are familiar with the symbolic meaning of this information as it arises, they may be able to find a clue as to what is happening during the process or indeed to what may be needed on a healing level in the future. However, the attunement will take place anyway, regardless of what is seen, felt or experienced. These types of experiences are simply the conscious manifestation of the movement of the energy as it clears blockages and creates the channel for the Reiki flow. I mention this because some students have latched onto this aspect as if it was in some way a determinant of how well the attunement was going. Some students have become almost obsessive about seeing lights, colors and other psychedelic stuff. As far as Reiki is concerned this is an irrelevance. There have been times however when, through sheer exasperation, I have almost felt like suggesting that taking drugs might be the answer if this is what they are looking for! I have so far managed to resist the urge.

The attunements can, either spontaneously or at a later time, release deep-seated emotions in the recipient. This can sometimes be uncomfortable as old fears, worries or feelings of anger surface for clearing. Some may burst into tears, whilst others break into a fit of what Lawrence Ellyard charmingly calls 'The Reiki Giggles'! Others may simply be in a state of very deep peace, but all will reach the point of glowing with positive feelings and energy. There is often a deep sense that with the Reiki attunements we are 'coming home' to our essential nature. Some students may develop enhanced intuitive abilities or find that there is an opening of the Third Eye and thus an expansion of latent psychic abilities. Of course the most obvious effect of the attunements and the one that they are universally characterized by is the ability to channel energy for the healing of oneself and others simply by the laying on of hands. As a consequence of receiving the 2nd Degree attunements this can also be done at a distance and the healing energy can be sent either forward or backward in time.

Reiki will always initiate a process of cleansing and detoxification within the physical body. This could be so mild, that it is hardly noticed by the student. For some it can be quite an ordeal. Various illnesses that may have been present in the students' past that had not been properly dealt with, may come back for final clearing. Headaches, nausea or dizziness can be quite common. It is comforting to know however, that these indicators of the start of the detoxification process are relatively short lived and often last only for the duration of the attunement process or for a little while after. Once the detox has taken place then the symptoms disappear of their own accord. Old habits, such as a reliance on alcohol or tobacco, or a particular type of food that is doing you no good, may also change. Once the attunement process is complete, the energy immediately goes to work on establishing a state of harmonious balance within the makeup of the student.

The opening of the Reiki channel takes place between the Crown and Heart *chakras*. However, the centers in the lower part of the body are just as important and so they too go through a corresponding adjustment in vibratory rate. It has been a traditional teaching within most branches of Reiki, and one that is born out by experience, that it takes about 21 days for the energy of the attunement to work through the entire body and *chakra* system, bringing a state of balance and increased vitality to all aspects of the body-mind. There will be times however when a particular student may have a great deal of detritus within them on various levels that needs to clear and this could and sometimes does take many months. Reiki will always guide you and help you at a pace that is comfortable for you at any given moment.

It is believed that by going through the Reiki attunement process, some of the *karmic* lessons of the individual are also lifted for good. Of course we may not be aware of what this *karma* is and what it had in store for us in any case, so it is not really worth pondering on to any great degree. Just be thankful that life's journey will become a little easier as a consequence!

## The Chakras and Nadis

Having brought up the subject of *chakras*, it may be worthwhile for the benefit of those readers who are not familiar with them, to take a brief look at what they are. I don't intend to go into this subject at any great length. There are dozens, possibly hundreds, of books that deal with this subject in a much more thorough and knowledgeable way than there is room for here. The *chakras* are however critical to the system of Reiki and the transmission through the body of this abundant healing and revitalizing energy.

According to the Hindu view of the human energy system, the human body has seven major and four subsidiary energy centers which are called *chakras*. Animals as well as humans have *chakras* and they are always to be found in the same locations from species to species relative to the functional layout of various body parts and organs. In ancient writings there are described many *chakras*, forty of which are thought to be of significance. *Chakra* is a Sanskrit word, meaning *wheel* and has been used since ancient times to describe the spinning vortices of energy of the human body. These centers of whirling energy can be visualized as projecting out from the physical body each with its own inherent color, which is dependent on its specific vibrational frequency. The colors of the *chakra* system are that of the rainbow. The seven main *chakras* are located as follows: on the crown of the head, in the center of the forehead (the third eye), the throat, in the center of the chest at the level of the heart, just above the navel, the sacrum and at the base of the spine. These *chakras* are connected to a fine channel of energy, which runs roughly parallel to the spinal chord. Each *chakra* is located where it can distribute vital energy to specific organs of the body. We each have many other *chakras*, but for our purposes we need only concern ourselves with these seven and two further energy centers located in the palms of the hands – the points from which the energy flows when we give a Reiki treatment to ourselves or another.

*Nadi* is another Sanskrit word that means *stream* or *river* and was applied by the ancient Indian sages to the energy channels that they perceived within the human body. *Nadis* are similar to acupuncture *meridians*. According to the ancient Indian system of health known as *Ayurveda* there are 72,000 *nadis* in the body and whilst located in the physical body they extend outwards to the various energy layers beyond. The *chakras* also extend out from the physical body to the universal body and are interconnected and interpenetrated by the *nadi* system.

The *chakras* can be perceived as funnels that connect the physical body to the various higher energy bodies, with each of these bodies having its own *chakra* system with its own corresponding frequency. This energetic web of *chakras* and *nadis* is vital to our existence as it allows for the transfer of information along the energy pathways between the various energy bodies and the physical body in the form of energetic vibrational patterns. Simply put, they serve as gateways for the flow of energy and life into our physical bodies, and thus the *chakras* and *nadis* play a vital role in the maintenance of our health and wellbeing by providing us with the vital energy that we need.

It is through the system of *chakras* and *nadis* that we are connected to the Universal Energy Field and it is the *nadis* that transfer energy from this infinite state of abundance to the physical body. The Reiki attunements increase the access to the Universal Energy Field by further opening the *nadi* channels and by increasing the vibrational frequency or 'spin' of the *chakras*. Thus as a consequence of the attunement process the energy of the Universal Energy Field has a much more unhindered passage through the *nadis* that originate in the crown *chakra* and that pass through the third eye, throat and heart *chakras* before dividing into two sub-channels that run down each arm to the palms and the palm *chakras*.

It is rarely mentioned in texts on the subtle energy system of the human body that the *chakras* and *nadis* are not fixed and immutable as one might suppose. Through the development of awareness in meditation or by the continual application of Reiki, it is possible to sense the *chakras* and *nadis* of your own energy system, and these may well be in different locations to the ones described in various texts on the subject. Because we are a dynamic system of continual energetic transmutation in an ever-changing energy field, we need to keep in mind that nothing is fixed and permanent. Your initial perceptions of energy movement and the location of various *nadis* and *chakras* may change as your awareness increases. The Buddhist concept regarding the perception of the *chakras* and *nadis* is that perception is conditioned and is a product of our consciousness. Our ability to perceive therefore is constantly changing as our consciousness itself is continually in a state of flux. As our ability to perceive energy changes, so too will the perceived location of the *chakras*. As we become more and more adept at bringing our minds to a state of focus and one-pointed concentration our perception of energy will become clearer. As a result we may start to sense the location of energetic elements within our makeup as being in the locations formerly described by those with highly developed perceptive abilities – the ancient sages who first identified the energetic map of the human body. The important thing is to rely on one's own inner vision in relation to the *chakras* and not to depend too much on the perceptions of others.

As well as distributing energy to physical organs within the body, the *chakras* also relate to specific aspects of human behavior and development. The lower *chakras*, at the base of the spine, the sacrum and above the navel, are associated with fundamental emotions and needs as the energy here vibrates at a lower frequency and is therefore somewhat crude in nature. The upper *chakras*, at the heart, throat, forehead (Third Eye) and crown, vibrate at a much higher frequency and correspond to our higher mental and spiritual aspirations.

By understanding the *chakras* we are able to fully appreciate and understand the relationship between our body and our consciousness. We can see that the body is a map of our consciousness. As each *chakra* represents not only physical aspects of our bodies but also particular aspects of our consciousness, we can become aware through our senses and perceptions that all possible states of awareness and everything that it is possible to experience can be divided into seven categories. Each category can be associated with a particular *chakra*. As we manifest emotions in our lives through our response to the conditions of life we can feel the effects of these emotions in the *chakras* associated with the part of the consciousness that is experiencing the emotions. We can also feel the effects in the physical parts of the body associated with the operative *chakra*. If a negative emotion stays with us for a length of time, through its effect on the relevant *chakra*, it can manifest physical problems in the associated parts of the body.

To affect a state of wellbeing we need to realize that each *chakra* needs to be balanced, clear, energized and properly spinning. When we can achieve this state the entire vibration of the physical body is raised. It is important therefore to open the *chakras* to increased energy flow. The more energy that flows, the better for our health on all levels. All illness is caused by an imbalance of energy, or a blocking of the flow of energy. The Reiki attunements and the continued application of Reiki can help us to restore this state of balance and thus bring harmony to all aspects of our lives.

Along with the commonly known translation of the word *chakra* as *wheel*, they are also often referred to and associated with the petals of a lotus flower. I have included this information in the following very brief outline of the correspondences and functions of the seven main *chakras,* as the *chakras* are often depicted in this form in a large number of texts on the subject. I have also given the Sanskrit name along with the Western version.

## The Base or Root Chakra (Mulhadara)
*Color:* Red (4 red petals)
*Associated endocrine gland:* Adrenals
*Associated perception or sense:* Kinaesthetic/physical
*Mulhadara* lies in the area of the coccyx in men and between the ovaries in women. It is the *chakra* that regulates the mechanisms that keep the physical body alive and is the seat of physical vitality and the primary urge to survive. Not only is this *chakra* a source of life force energy, it is also the vital foundation for all of the other *chakras* as well as the seat of the collective unconscious, and is the gateway through which this becomes accessible.

## The Sacral or Sexual Chakra (Svadisthana)
*Color:* Orange (6 orange petals)
*Associated endocrine gland:* Gonads
*Associated perception or sense:* Feeling
*Svadisthana* is located just below the navel in front of the sacrum. This is the center of sexual energy and of the ego. This is where we open to others, particularly the opposite sex. It is the body's center of gravity and is often called *the sea of energy*. The Chinese refer to it as the *Tan T'ien* and the Japanese as the *Hara*.

**The Solar Plexus or Navel Chakra (Manipura)**
*Color:* Yellow (10 yellow petals)
*Associated endocrine gland:* Pancreas
*Associated perception or sense:* Emotion
Located slightly above the navel, this *chakra* is the center of the body from which physical energy is distributed. This is the center of unrefined emotions and of our gut instinct, which influences how we relate to others and the wider world. Our personality is shaped here as we assimilate feelings and experiences from the world around us. This *chakra* is also associated with power, strength, abundance and wisdom.

**The Heart Chakra (Anahata)**
*Color:* Green/Pink (12 emerald green petals)
*Associated endocrine gland:* Thymus
*Associated perception or sense:* Love/empathy
Located at the height of the heart in the center of the chest. The unconditional love that we work with in healing develops and flows from here. Feelings of intimacy, love/loss of love, joy and sadness, compassion, affection, devotion and selflessness are all felt in and emanate from this *chakra*. It is the center of real unconditional love. It also affects the heart, the lungs, the respiratory system and the immune system.

The heart *chakra* is the central *chakra* in our system of seven. Symbolically within the 12 petaled lotus there are two interlacing equilateral triangles forming a six-pointed star. These triangles represent matter rising to spirit and thus liberation, and spirit descending into manifestation on the physical level. The six-pointed star symbolizes the perfect balance of the two polarities of body and spirit creating a center of peace. To fully open the heart *chakra* we need to establish balance between the various aspects of our existence, such as male and female, mind and body, light and shadow and practicality and spirituality.

## The Throat Chakra (Vishuddha)
*Color:* Blue (16 blue petals)
*Associated endocrine gland:* Thyroid
*Associated perception or sense:* Communication/hearing/speaking
This *chakra* governs our need to communicate with others and the rest of the world, and is located between the inner collarbone and larynx. Our creative and expressive urges spring from this energy center and it is also where we perceive our own inner voice and those coming from other realms. It is the access point to more subtle levels of being.

## The Brow or Third Eye chakra (Ajna)
*Color:* Indigo (96 blue/violet petals – often shown as 2 petals only)
*Associated endocrine gland:* Pituitary
*Associated perception or sense:* Seeing/visualization
Located in the middle of the forehead, this is the seat of extra-sensory perceptions such as clairvoyance and telepathy. It is also the location of our will, intellect and spirit. The Third Eye is our eye of wisdom and corresponds to spiritual awakening in many mystic traditions. We visualize things here, and thus some of the functions of this *chakra* are realization, intuition, the development of the inner senses and the projection of our will.

## The Crown or Lotus Chakra (Sahasrara)
*Color:* White/violet (1000 violet petals)
*Associated endocrine gland:* Pineal
*Associated perception or sense:* Spiritual
This *chakra* is located at the top of the head at the fontanel. Here we have the entry point for the flow of Universal Energy: *ki/chi/prana*, and it is the seat of our direct spiritual vision through which we can achieve the highest level of consciousness, that of enlightenment. When working with this *chakra* we are involved in advanced spiritual development that will ultimately lead to unity with the All/God, or the attainment of Cosmic Consciousness.

# 3

## *The History of Reiki*
# Part 1: Mikao Usui

Love is not an emotion, it is your very existence.
*Sri Ravi Shankar*

Telling the history of Reiki is a bit like trying to strain spaghetti through a tennis racket – just when you think that you've got it all, half of it slips away through the holes. Shake it a bit and more slips off. Pinning down the history of Reiki is becoming a major preoccupation for many people in the Reiki community these days, as the story gets more and more convoluted each time a new piece of information is unearthed. Often contradictions arise, and to make matters worse, some unscrupulous people are trying to pass off so-called 'channelled' information as historical fact. This of course just leaves us all in a mess, not knowing what to believe, or what sources to trust.

The question of whether the history of Reiki really matters anyway does often arise. Ultimately, the answer is obviously 'no' it doesn't. The important thing is the teaching, and the practice, and how we relate to the world and other beings as a consequence of this practice, but we are simply human, and thus have a connection with what has gone before and what will come after us. It is a part of being human to be curious, and frankly there is no harm in this, as long as we can keep it all in the right perspective, and ultimately improve ourselves by just getting on with our spiritual practice of Reiki. But let's just unravel some of this spaghetti before it all slips through the holes.

I have limited myself to a perusal of that part of the history of Reiki that is particularly pertinent to the lineage of Reiki Jin Kei Do. There are now many streams of Reiki, often dating back to some of the prime movers within the development of the system, and it is not appropriate here to go into the detail of these various histories as they relate to individual members of the Reiki family. This information for those that require it is available in a number of other books and on various websites. A warning though: as I said, the history of Reiki is a work-in-progress, and as such some of this material may change in time.

## Mikao Usui

It was Mikao Usui, a Japanese Tendai Buddhist who developed the original spiritual system that we have come to know as Reiki. In the early days it was known as *Usui Do,* a name given to the system by Usui's students. Usui himself imply referred to it as *My Method* or as one student has claimed *Method to Achieve Personal Perfection.*

## His Life and Times

Reiki or *Usui Do* as we shall call it for the time being was born into the world at a time in Japanese history when major sociological changes were taking place in its political and cultural life. Japan was beginning to open up to the world after two centuries of self-imposed isolation, and massive industrialization was starting to transform the country from a feudal society to a major industrial nation, capable of competing with the West on an equal footing.

Little did Usui realize that he was creating a system of spiritual practice that was, in less than a century, going to take the world by storm – or at least, for the time being, that part of it that realized that there was more to life than the frenetic pursuit of money and materialism. But let's go back a little to Usui's early life.

Mikao Usui was born into a wealthy Tendai Buddhist family which was descended from one of the most famous and influential *Samurai* families in all of Japan; the Chiba clan, on 15 August 1865 in the village of Tanai Mura (now called Miyama-cho) in the Yamagata district of the Gifu Prefecture of Kyoto – the former Japanese capital. He had two brothers, Sanya and Kuniji and one sister called Tsuru. The family were very much a part of the Japanese nobility, which was a reflection of their background and ancestry in one of the higher *Samurai* ranks, that of *Hatamoto*. The *Hatamoto Samurai* had been the *Shogun's* personal guard. The bearer of this rank was entitled to have retainers, hold land and station in life and carry two swords, not that this highly privileged position would necessarily and ultimately do the young Mikao Usui much good in his passage through life. The *Samurai* classes were under attack by the prevailing social order at that time. Six years after his birth a decree was passed banning *Samurai* from carrying swords, followed six years later by the final quelling of the last *Samurai* uprising. A new social and political order was beginning to flex its muscles in Japan, that of the Meiji (meaning *enlightened government*) Restoration, lead by Prince Mutsuhito who in 1868 became the 122nd Emperor of Japan.

At the age of four, Usui entered a Tendai Buddhist monastery near Mt Kurama (*Horse Saddle Mountain*) to begin a period of several years of intensive training in this school of Mikkyo Buddhism (the other school being Shingon). Usui's commitment to Tendai led him for a short while in later life to become a Tendai Buddhist monk or priest (similar to a lay priest), but maintaining his own home rather than living in a temple. In Japanese this is known as a *zaike* – a priest possessing a home. It was at this time that Usui took on his Buddhist name of *Gyoho* (or *Gyohan* or *Gyotse*).

With the restoration of rule by Emperor in 1868, when Usui was only three years old, Mutsuhito, who reigned until 1912, was determined to bring about a modern, outward-looking and dynamic new focus to his country, and mark a new beginning in Japanese history. To this end he encouraged his subjects to go out and study the ways of the West. Usui, having a strong fascination for all things Western was, as he grew up, more than happy to oblige. Over the span of his life he traveled extensively, visiting the US and Europe several times as well as China to study and learn the Western ways. He was always a hard working student and accumulated a vast knowledge of medicine, psychology, fortune telling and the theology of world religions. Much of his study of the latter may well have taken place in the University Library in Kyoto where sacred texts from all over the world were held. He also studied Chinese Traditional Medicine, numerology, astrology and psychic and clairvoyant development.

Usui was something of an eccentric by all accounts, and as a young man had faced more than his fair share of adversity it seems, having no regular employment or security and frequently suffering from a lack of money. This however seems to have been a conscious decision by Usui, who did not place any real value on material possessions. Over the years he followed a number of professions: industrialist, missionary, reporter, office worker, public servant and supervisor of convicts. At one point in his life (possibly 1921) he worked as a 'private secretary' (for this read 'bodyguard'!) for Goto Shimpei who was the Head of the Department for Health and Welfare and the former head of the civil administration of Taiwan and later Mayor of Tokyo. It would seem that Usui possessed some of the essential qualities needed by a professional bodyguard, as shown in this description of him by one of his students:

> He was physically big, quiet in manner and extremely
> powerful. (He) did not accept fools willingly and could be quite
> abrasive at times. He could get righteously angry and quite

impatient, particularly with people who wanted results but were not prepared to work for them.

Usui did manage to find time amongst his various work and study commitments to marry Sadako Suzuki sometime shortly after the turn of the 20th century, and in 1908 his son Fuji was born, followed in 1913 by his daughter Toshiko. Fuji went on to teach at Tokyo University. He died on 1946. Toshiko had a short life and died at the age of 22 in 1935.

It is claimed within the traditional histories of Reiki that are told in the West, that following the development of his spiritual discipline, Usui went on to spend several years doing healing work in the beggar's quarter of Kyoto. There is little evidence to substantiate this but the story may well refer to Usui's experience of working with the victims of one of Japan's most devastating natural disasters.

In 1923 the Kanto Earthquake struck, 50 miles from Tokyo. The ensuing devastation completely destroyed both Tokyo and Yokohama with an estimated 140,000 people either dead or missing. It was not the most powerful earthquake that Japan had ever experienced but the ensuing destruction made it the greatest natural disaster in Japanese history. Usui dedicated himself to treating the victims of this terrible event, and as a consequence in recognition of his services, he was apparently awarded an honorary doctorate (it is claimed that this is why he is known as Dr Usui. Though others have suggested that this was merely a mistranslation of *sensei* (a respectful term for teacher) in the West, and that he was never referred to as a doctor in Japan. His understanding of medicine was based upon his own research. He was never formally trained in medicine). His memorial stone states that he "reached out his hands of love to suffering people" during the emergency.

Mikao Usui eventually died from a stroke – his third – whilst on a visit to Fukuyama, Hiroshima on the 9th March 1926. His ashes are buried at the Pure Land Buddhist Saihoji Temple in the suburbs of Tokyo with his entire family where a memorial was erected to his memory by his student Rear Admiral Ushida in 1927. The memorial also acknowledges Usui's critical *satori* experience, which is often mentioned in the history of the development of Usui's system as having taken place on Mt Kurama. A family tomb was also constructed on this site by Usui's son Fuji in the same year. Some of Usui's remains were placed in a private shrine at his training center, along with his portrait, lit by two oil lamps and the copy of the five Reiki Precepts that had hung there. The Precepts were brushed by Usui's own hand in 1921.

## Ingredients of the Usui Do Soup

It is highly likely that what Usui learnt following his attendance at the Tendai monastery at the age of four eventually provided the fundamental underpinnings of the *Usui Do* system. It is possible that Mikkyo Buddhism, which has many associations with an esoteric practice called Shugendo (which translates as 'the way of cultivating psychic and spiritual powers') also informed his system. Shugendo was a blend of pre-Buddhist folk traditions, Tantric Buddhism, Chinese Yin-Yang magic and Taoism. It is a tradition that involves strict ascetic mystical disciplines such as fasting, long periods of isolation, meditation and the use of incantations and *mudra* like techniques to achieve the state of *kantoku* (illuminating mystical visionary states) to gain spiritual empowerment. These practices imbued the *Yamabushi* (itinerant mountain priests) with such powers as healing, exorcism, clairsentience and the ability to master the effects of extreme heat and cold. Certainly Usui would have had considerable exposure to these types of practices and consequent abilities and may well have mastered some if not all of them himself. Of course we are well aware of his mastery of the ability to heal the self and others.

Possibly influenced by his family's *Samurai* background, it is believed that at the age of 12, Usui began training in a martial art with a pronounced Zen feel to it called *Yagyu Shinkage Ryu* which incorporated *Ken-Jutsu* (*Samurai* swordsmanship) and *Ju-Jutsu* (unarmed combat). During his 20s he finally achieved his teachers licence (called *Menkyo Kaiden*) for this martial art which marked his proficiency in weaponry and grappling at the highest level. This system includes techniques for both life taking and life giving (*sappo* and *kappo*) and an exercise called *katsu*, a method for infusing life energy into a person. It is said that Usui also studied at about this time another martial art called *Aiki Jutsu*. Such was Usui's standing in the martial arts community that it seems that he was known and very well respected by other giants in the field such as Morihei Ueshiba, the founder of *Aikido*, Jigoro Kano, the founder of Japanese *Judo* and Gichin Kunakoshi, the founder of *Karate* — not an insignificant group of martial arts luminaries! It has been suggested that Usui achieved high levels of proficiency in a variety of ancient Japanese methods including *Ki Ko*, the Japanese version of *Qi Gong* (energy cultivation), and consequently practised the technique of *Ki Ko* projection healing.

It has been claimed that he was also very much involved in a spiritualist/healing group called *Rei Jyutsu Kai* which was attended by some of the most gifted and spiritual monks, nuns, psychics and clairvoyants in Japan (very much as it is today). Some of the claims made for Usui's involvement in various spiritual and/or martial systems may be speculative to some degree or another, but what we do know is that he did have a strong and overriding desire to pursue the Truth to discover the ultimate meaning of life and so find the way to escape from suffering. He seemed more than willing to explore whatever method might lead him to it. For three years, starting in about 1918/19 he also had a dalliance with Zen Buddhism. He was above all else a man with a mission. How much any of his studies in the various spiritual, martial and energetic systems contributed to the development of *Usui Do* is again open to speculation to some degree, but it is certain that all, in shaping the man, must have contributed to it in some way either consciously or unconsciously. It is easy to see many strands within modern Reiki that can be traced back to possible and in some cases certain origins in the systems that Usui studied.

In searching for the Truth, Usui began to put together his system for personal and spiritual liberation. As a Tendai Buddhist, he drew heavily on the teachings of this tradition to provide the spiritual backbone or foundation to his practice. Elements of Shintoism were included that provided the methods for controlling and working with the energies. It is also highly likely that his experiences in *Yagyu Shinkage Ryu* and *Ki Ko* contributed in some way to the overall blend. Perhaps there are other sources too. From the evidence of the teachings within the lineage of Reiki Jin Kei Do, it seems more than likely that he also drew on the spiritual practice that is now known as *Buddho-EnerSense*, because the origins and deeper meanings of the Reiki symbols are contained within this system. Usui had much to draw on from his numerous studies and mastery of a number of disciplines. Perhaps Shugendo, which seems to have a strong resonance with Reiki also contributed in some way. Perhaps we shall never really know all of the ingredients that go to make up the Reiki, or *Usui Do* soup.

## Mountain Retreat

One of the most often talked about and critical factors in the development of the *Usui Do* system is Usui's experience of satori, also known as an absorptive (*dhyanic*) state, on Mt Kurama. As well as being the place where mountain spirits are said to have given the secrets of fighting to the *Samurai*, which Usui would clearly have an ancestral affinity for, Mt Kurama has been described as 'the spiritual heart of Japan' and as such has been visited by countless numbers of people in search of enlightenment and the meaning of life, Usui simply being one amongst this number. For many years in the West, the story of the development of Reiki has hinged on this event. The story goes that in his search for the ultimate Truth, Usui decided to fast and meditate for 21 days (this practice is known as *kushu shinren* – a form of *shyu gyo* – which means a painful or difficult training). His hopes of having this Truth revealed to him were realized and on the last day he experienced a moment of *satori* – this being Usui's empowerment to the Universal Life Force Energy. Although some claim that no such meditation retreat took place as none of Usui's students and contemporaries mention it, we do know that in 1914 (some have claimed it was as late as 1920) he travelled to Mt Kurama and apparently enrolled in a 21-day training course called *Isyu Guo*. No details of the training are available, however it is likely to have involved fasting, meditation, chanting and prayers, and it would in any case seem highly unlikely that Usui did not from time to time engage in meditative retreats of this kind. Even today serious searchers for the Truth meditate on Mt Kurama where there is a small waterfall under which people stand to allow the waters to strike and flow over the top of their heads, a practice that is said to activate the crown *chakra*. It is possible that Usui performed this meditation, as many Japanese Reiki Masters believe, as a part of his practice.

The holy mountain of Kurama is known to have been the home of a branch of the Tendai Buddhist sect (their main temple being on Mt Hiei just outside Kyoto), and for a time the spiritualist group *Rei Jyutsu Kai* that Usui is reported to have been a member of, had a base at the foot of the mountain (the site now being occupied by another group). Most commentators on the development of Reiki acknowledge that Usui did experience *satori* during the *Isyu Guo* meditative retreat on the mountain (possibly under the waterfall) at which point the great Reiki energy entered his crown *chakra*. Usui's system was certainly already in place and being taught to others by the time of the meditation retreat, but his powerful and ecstatic enlightenment experience must have been critical to the development of the system as we know it today.

Over recent years as more and more of the history of Reiki as we formally knew it has been jettisoned in the wake of new research evidence, it has become increasingly difficult to find references to the beautiful description given of Usui's *satori* experience. Presumably this has been consigned to the dustbin of 'make believe' along with much material that rightly deserves to have been jettisoned. This description is possibly important however. It was nicely described by Bodo Baginski and Shalila Sharamon in their book *Reiki Universal Life Energy:*

> (Usui)...saw a shining light moving towards him with great speed. It became bigger and bigger and finally hit him in the middle of the forehead. Dr. Usui...suddenly saw millions of little bubbles in...all the colors of the rainbow.

What is being described here, it would seem, is an experience of *tigle* (or *bindu* in Hindi). *Tigle* is the Tibetan word that describes vital essence drops or spheres of psychic energy that are visualized and manifest due to the practice of deep and profound meditation, and is a critical experience within the Vajrayana/Tantric Buddhist traditions. *Tigle* represents the mind aspect of experience and either sits in a *chakra* or is visualized passing along energy channels within the body. *Tigle* are directly related to the movement of energy and to the functioning of the mind. The metaphor often used is that of the mind being a lame rider and the *prana* or *ki* (*chi*) being a blind horse. The *ki* has no direction without the mind, whilst the mind has no capacity to move without the *ki*. They function as a unit, and the *tigle* is the rider of the *pranic* horse.

It is my belief that Usui, in being an experienced meditator of the highest order, was undergoing an experience of the spontaneous manifestation of *tigle* related to the energy empowerment that he sought.

Many people involved in researching the history of Reiki have suggested that the meditation engaged in by Usui on Mt Kurama that lead to the *satori* experience and the entering of the Reiki energy through his crown *chakra* is one that is derived from Tendai Buddhism called *The Lotus Repentance*. However, in the lineage of Reiki Jin Kei Do it is claimed that Usui performed the first three cycles of a meditation, now known as *Buddho*. *Buddho* means 'energy' or 'seed' of enlightenment. This meditation was the spark that would later send a Zen monk by the name of Seiji Takamori in search of the roots of the Reiki system. The *Buddho* meditation is known to have been passed on by Usui who had received it from a monk who had advised him to practice the meditation in order to receive the energy empowerments that he sought. This cyclic meditation involved a direct connection to and visualisation of Buddhist deities and symbols that are the root of one of the widely known Reiki symbols. What is not entirely clear is just how much of this meditation Usui was aware of. He may well have known more than just the first three cycles, though this assertion is open to speculation to a degree.

## Usui Teaches His System

It is not entirely clear exactly when Usui began to teach his system to others. The general consensus is that it was around 1914/15, although one source suggests that as early as 1912 Usui was engaged in a process of formalizing his training programme, thus implying that it could have been being taught in an informal manner even earlier than this. We do know that one student, a Tendai Buddhist nun and cousin of his wife, known as Suzuki san studied with him from 1915 until 1920. What is absolutely clear however is that at this early stage Usui did not devise nor did he teach a hands-on healing system. This came much later, towards the end of his life. The system that he developed was for the spiritual development and ultimate liberation from suffering of the individual, in fact self-healing, though not necessarily by the laying on of hands. As a by-product of this system he also created a method for the healing of others. At no time was this intended to be the focus of the system that Usui taught. This aspect of the system was later expanded upon by others, most notably one of Usui's last students before he died – Chujiro Hayashi.

It is not known exactly how many students Usui trained. His memorial stone at Saihoji Temple in Tokyo suggests that it was in the order of 2000 people. Following Japanese custom however, this figure should be interpreted to simply mean a large number, though some have suggested that Usui may well have trained in excess of 1000 people. It is claimed that up until the last 18 months of his life Usui only trained those from a Buddhist or Shinto background. Very few of his students, perhaps only a handful, would have made it through to the higher levels of the system, but it still proved to be very popular with the older generation who saw Usui's teachings as a return to the older spiritual practices and values at a time of great social change in Japan.

Much is not known or only half understood about what constituted a particular teaching under Usui. He does not seem to have used what we might consider as being a 'formal' system of training at all, with a precisely defined set of teachings. Following the standard practices in the teaching of Buddhist methods, Usui only passed on what he felt to be appropriate for a particular student, adding and omitting material where necessary. This might perhaps explain why there often seems to be anomalies between the accounts given to us by various people who studied with Usui. It is highly likely that they were given only those teachings that were most appropriate to them, and other teachings, which were not considered to be appropriate being left out. In the modern Western traditions of Reiki there were originally significant omissions when compared to what we now know of Usui's teachings. More and more material is surfacing all of the time, and many Western Reiki Masters are now trying to re-introduce some of Usui's material, or what is believed to be Usui's material (but may well have been added by others) into their classes. *Usui Do* in its original form was not divided into three degrees as is modern-day Reiki. There was an open-ended commitment to study, not a fixed length training course, and it was only when you had developed sufficiently that you were invited to move on to the higher levels. Usui's approach to training has also in recent times been revitalized in the West, and there are now one or two schools teaching the system in this manner, including the use of regular weekly *reiju* empowerments that Usui first began to use in 1922 (very different to the one-off attunement processes that we are so familiar with today) and the grading system that he introduced in 1923 based on that established by Jigoro Kano (the creator of *Judo*). These levels were: *Rokkyu, Gokyu, Yonkyu, Sankyu, Nikkyu* (Power symbol taught at this level), *Ikkyu* (Mental/Emotional symbol taught), *Shodan* (Distant symbol taught), *Nidan* (Master symbol taught), *Sandan, Yondan, Godan, Rokudan* and *Shichidan*. This grading system was in use until late 1925.

It was in April 1922 that Usui opened his first 'seat of learning' in Harajuku, Aoyama, Tokyo and used a small training manual that had come into use in about 1920. It did not contain any hand positions for treating others, but did contain the *gokai* (moral precepts or principles) that were first introduced to the system in April 1921, meditations and the *Waka* poetry of the Meiji Emperor. His motto for the center was "Unity of self through harmony and balance." Usui used the center as a base from which to teach his spiritual system and also to offer healing to those in need. In February 1924 following the Kanto Earthquake, the training center was moved to larger premises in a suburban house in Nakano, outside Tokyo, the site being arrived at through the process of divination.

Of those that Usui taught, about 50 to 70 of them went on to achieve what we would now consider to be the first level of 2nd Degree, and maybe 30 or so went on to the second level of 2nd Degree. It is claimed that 21 people ultimately went on to achieve *Shinpiden* (Masters) level.

Usui's teachings were called a *Ronin* (leaderless) method. This was to ensure that no one would try to monopolize his system, and that it would remain freely available to all those who wanted it.

## Some Key Students

The 21 students that achieved the level of *Shinpiden* included amongst others five Buddhist nuns, three naval officers and nine other men. One of these was Usui's best friend and senior student Toshihiro Eguchi, a school teacher who reportedly went on to teach thousands of students across Japan (though according to Hiroshi Doi of *The Usui Reiki Ryoho Gakkai*, Eguchi only studied the first levels of the *Usui Do* system). Eguchi spent several months training with Usui in 1920/21 and also some suggest from 1925 to 1927, firstly with Usui and then with his school. It is through his lineage that the majority of Reiki has continued in Japan. In 1928, after Usui's death, Eguchi formed his own school called *Eguchi Tenohira Ryoji Kenkyu-kai*, and in 1930 published his own manual *Tenohira Ryoji Nyumon* (An Introduction to Healing with the Palms). A further book was published in 1954 called *Te No Hira Ryoji Wo Kataru* (A Story of Healing With the Palms). It is believed that at some point in his life, and for several years he ran a healing community called *Ittoen*. He was also later to found his own religion, which is still followed today, and is a form of Shinto-revivalism. It includes as a part of its practice, initiation procedures and hands-on healing techniques. Eguchi was in fact already practising a form of hand healing when he met Usui, and later would teach some of his techniques to Usui's students when he returned to Usui's training center in 1923. By this point some of Usui's teachings had been incorporated into Eguchi's system, which also seems to have developed strong religious overtones and a blessing ceremony. Usui was not entirely comfortable with Eguchi's approach, but allowed him to teach at his center twice a week in order to support his income. The techniques taught by Eguchi are very similar to those practised by another of Usui's students – the man who was eventually to become the catalyst for the world wide spread of Reiki, Chujiro Hayashi. It is possible, if not highly likely, that some of what Hayashi learnt and later passed on came directly from Eguchi, who continued to teach

*Usui Do* alongside his own system. It has been recently speculated that perhaps Eguchi had a much bigger influence on the style of Reiki that eventually emerged in the West than had previously been realized. If Eguchi did only study the basic levels of Usui's system as Hiroshi Doi claims, then it seems remarkable that a novice should have such a seemingly profound influence on the direction of the *Usui Do* system.

In 1925, soon after moving his training center to Nakano, Usui came across a group of Imperial Officers who were to become his students, including Rear Admirals Jusaburo Ushida, Kan'ichi Taketomi and Naval Captain Chujiro Hayashi. This however was only after a period of some resistance from others amongst Usui's students who did not think it appropriate that such a system should be taught to military men. It would appear that there might well have been some arm-twisting taking place to finally get Usui to pass on his teachings to them. Usui's system had come to the attention of the Japanese Navy. Whilst possessing very modern and well-equipped ships, they had only limited medical equipment and personnel and so were keen to find any method that could be used as a form of emergency treatment. Usui's method was what they wanted. Hayashi and the other naval officers were not particularly interested in the spiritual aspects of the system, preferring to focus on the treatment side, which was considerably less important from Usui's point of view. As a consequence of theirs and the Navy's interest there seems to have been something of a shift in the structure and nature of the training at Usui's center. A substantially different form of energy work began to emerge, with its focus on treating others rather than oneself. It was this system that was the forerunner of modern Reiki. Incorporated into this were Eguchi's healing concepts and his blessing ceremony, along with *Ki Ko* (*Qi Gong*) techniques also derived from Eguchi. It was at this point that a new grading system also came into use. Four new levels were introduced: *Shoden* (first grade), *Chuuden* (middle grade), *Okuden* (inner grade) and *Kaiden* (explanation grade). All former grades above *Nidan* were dropped. The grading system would ultimately change a number of times under the influence of subsequent students until it eventually evolved into the three-degree format that we have today.

It has been suggested that Hayashi (and some have suggested possibly the two other officers) initially had some trouble experiencing the energies and so Usui was forced to modify the system and in conjunction with his senior student Eguchi introduced the symbols to his practice that are so familiar to Western Reiki practitioners. These were to be used as a focusing device to increase sensitivity to energy flow. This assertion however raises many questions over the nature of Usui's training prior to this. Surely Chujiro Hayashi was not the first student to have problems over sensing the energies?  We already have established that the symbols were an integral part of the training as laid down in the levels based upon Kano's *Judo* system that were introduced in 1923 and so were clearly in use long before the naval officers arrived on the scene and thus before Usui's system developed more of a therapeutic bias. It is worth also reflecting briefly on the nature of the Reiki symbols. The Reiki symbols are complex meditative devices, that whilst they do increase sensitivity to energy flow, have many more uses and meanings beyond this simplistic way of approaching them. As Usui had built a system for personal spiritual liberation, it is unlikely that he would introduce a device that had as its major contribution to the system nothing more than an application in Reiki Therapeutics. Whatever the truth of this Hayashi, Ushida and Taketomi were the last people to be taught by Usui. It is claimed that Usui referred to these three as *ryuku*, which means someone who is a good practitioner, but not familiar with the full teachings. Again there seems to be an anomaly here, as it is known that Hayashi was one of only two of Usui's students to reach the very highest levels of training in the system (*Shichidan*), he was clearly not a run-of-the-mill student, in spite of having only trained with Usui for a period of about six to nine months. Perhaps his level of achievement refers only

to his study of the healing aspects of the system, whilst the label
*ryuku* denotes the fact that he did not receive in any great depth
the spiritual teachings.

There have been reports that possibly two Buddhist nuns also
achieved the level of attainment that would qualify them to be
awarded the *Shichidan* grade, but it was customary at that time in
Japan for women not to be awarded the highest level.

As an interesting side note in the evolution of Reiki, it has
been claimed by the still-living cousin of Usui's wife Suzuki san,
that in early 1925, *Usui Do* metamorphosed into a new form
called *Usui Teate* (Usui Hand/Palm Healing). This apparently
was taught by Eguchi under the guidance of Usui himself, and
is said to be Usui's own application of the *Usui Do* system. It is
focused on the personal liberation of the practitioner through a
series of exercises and other practices. These practices and much
of the systems underpinning philosophy seems to be grounded
in Mikkyo Buddhism (Mikkyo is the name given to the Japanese
Buddhist philosophic system, the two main schools of which are
Tendai and Shingon). Mikkyo, which means 'secret teaching' is an
esoteric practice built up in much the same way that Usui built up
*Usui Do*; from a wide variety of philosophies, teachings, mantras,
rituals, meditation techniques, deities etc, but draws extensively
on Mahayana (Vajrayana) Buddhism. It is becoming clearer that
Usui's original system may have had its origins, in part at least, in
a tradition of Buddhist thought and practice that seems to share
the same or similar roots to that system re-discovered by Seiji
Takamori in the Himalayas.

# 4

## *The History of Reiki*
## Part 2: Beyond Usui

What lies behind us and what lies before us are tiny matters compared to what lies within us.

*Oliver Wendell Holmes*

### Chujiro Hayashi
### A Military Man Changes Direction

Chujiro Hayashi, a committed practitioner of Soto Zen Buddhism was born in Tokyo on 15 September 1880. He graduated from naval school in 1902 and by the time that he was doing his Masters training with Usui in 1925, he was 45 years old, a former Director of Ominato Port Defense Station at the foot of Mt Osore in northern Japan, Captain of the Imperial Navy, a naval doctor and married with two children. His son Tadayoshi was born in 1903 followed by his daughter Kiyoe in 1910. As Hayashi was one of only two students (the other being Eguchi) to be awarded the level of *Shichidan* by Usui, he must clearly have been one of Usui's most senior students (at least it would seem, in terms of the healing aspects of the system). Probably in part as a consequence of the high levels of attainment in the Usui system that Hayashi had reached, he was given the *Buddho* meditation, which Usui had practiced on Mt Kurama. It is not known if this meditation was also passed on to Eguchi, perhaps it was a part of the teachings available to anyone who had attained the highest levels. Whether Hayashi practised the meditation or not is also unclear but certainly the system of *Usui Do*/Reiki was to become the defining anthem of the rest of his life.

## From Usui Do to Reiki

As a consequence of his former role as a naval doctor and thus being imbued with the sensibilities of the medical profession, Hayashi, upon completion of his training with Usui, opened an eight-bed Reiki clinic at his home, employing up to 20 practitioners, and began to use the Usui system as a therapeutic healing method. Clients were always treated by two or more people at a time, and Hayashi kept detailed records of all the treatments that were given in the clinic. He wanted to see if the system would fit the traditional medical model when used as a healing therapy. The information that he collected was used to formulate a set of standard hand positions for different ailments so that upon diagnosis, a particular treatment pattern could be used to treat the condition. His research in this area was undertaken whilst Usui was still alive and with his approval. Usui wanted to see if his system of spiritual development could stand alone as a healing method. Hayashi's approach was a long way from Usui's much more intuitive understanding of healing which was not dominated by the requirement to place your hands on another person to effect healing, though Usui did teach five hand positions based around treating the head during the 1920s.

The information that Hayashi collected was ultimately published as a manual called *Ryoho Shishin* and added to the already existing notes of the system, the whole being called the *Usui Reiki Ryoho Hikkei*. The resultant manual was produced at Usui's request, and was used by him with his own students. It is interesting to note that the *Usui Reiki Ryoho Hikkie* had dropped the meditation material that had originally appeared in Usui's earlier manual of around 1920, and thus confirms that the system of *Usui Do* was undergoing a process of reorientation under Hayashi to a form of energy therapy rather than as a self-development tool.

Following Usui's death in 1926, Hayashi, Ushida and Taketomi moved Usui's training center to nearby the Hayashi Reiki clinic in the Shinano Machi district. Ushida and Taketomi then went on to form the *Usui Reiki Ryoho Gakkai* (Usui Reiki Healing Method Society) as a sort of memorial society. This is based in Tokyo and is still in existence today. Hayashi, although not directly involved in establishing the *Gakkai*, was a member from its inception and Mikao Usui was named as the notional and honorary 1st President of the society. The work of the *Gakkai* very much emphasized the use of Reiki as a healing system, as all students were given a copy of the *Usui Reiki Ryoho Hikkei* to guide their studies. One of Hayashi's own Master students and another naval officer, Tatsumi, who trained with Hayashi from 1927 to 1931, has referred to the *Gakkai* rather disparagingly as 'an officers club'. It wasn't long after the formation of this group under the guidance of Ushida and Taketomi, that it started to develop a strong nationalistic flavor, which was anathema to Hayashi who found that this did not sit well with his own beliefs. *Ki Ko* (*Qi Gong*) techniques that were not in keeping with Usui's original teachings also became much more prominent, and so in 1931 Hayashi left.

It would seem that the word 'Reiki' (and *Reiki Ryoho*) as a label for Hayashi's modified Usui system was first used by Hayashi and his naval associates. None of Usui's surviving former students are familiar with the term 'Reiki'. As a term denoting a form of spiritual healing however, 'Reiki' had been used by a number of other therapists prior to this and was not specific to Usui's system or the modified derivatives that followed. The Usui system has now become largely synonymous with the term 'Reiki' as a result of the understandable assumptions of Western practitioners that the name only referred to Usui's practice, not realizing that it was a generic term for many similar disciplines.

## Hayashi Goes It Alone

In 1930, prior to his departure from the *Gakkai*, Dr Hayashi founded his own healing society called *Hayashi Reiki Ryoho Kenkyu-kai* (The Hayashi Reiki Research Center). His wife Chie acted as the Center's receptionist and hostess. Hayashi was in the process of moving further and further away from *Usui Do* as a method to achieve personal liberation to Reiki as a method of hands-on healing. More aspects of Usui's teachings were changed, but these did not prove to be popular. A 40-page manual was produced for his students that listed a complex series of hand positions for various ailments. It would appear that at some point Hayashi abandoned this approach however, and introduced the concept of free positioning of the hands. By the time that Hayashi left the *Gakkai* he had pretty much abandoned the original *Usui Do* system.

As Hayashi moved away from the Usui model, some of his own senior students, including Tatsumi, began to leave the school in frustration at the divergence between what Hayashi was now teaching and the teachings that had been passed on to him by Usui. In addition to the primary focus of the system, Hayashi also changed the way the system was taught. It was Hayashi who modified and systematized Usui's teachings and created the standard hand positions, the system of three degrees and their initiation procedures, which is pretty much the system of Reiki that the West finally inherited. The 1st Degree was taught over a 5-day period, with each day's training taking about three hours, followed by a practical session in which students gave treatments and applied what they had learnt. According to Tatsumi and another of Hayashi's students, Mrs Chiyoko Yamaguchi (who studied the first two levels with Hayashi between 1938 and 1940 and ultimately went on to establish *Jikiden Reiki*), students would receive the attunements from Hayashi during these sessions, which seem to have been a significantly modified form of Usui's *reiju* empowerments, that may have been taught to Hayashi by Eguchi when the latter joined the *Gakkai* for a year out of respect for Usui (Eguchi then left the *Gakkai* due to the evident nationalism of some of the members).

The *Gakkai* does not use the Hayashi/Western attunement process however, but the original Usui-style *reiju*, which does not include the use of symbols or mantras, nor does it change form as the student progresses through the levels as is the case in the Western attunement process. Although the *Gakkai* are aware of the symbols and mantras used in the West, they do not form a part of their own teachings and are, like the attunement process, specific to the Hayashi lineages. It is interesting to note that there does seem to be some variation in the look of the Reiki symbols when comparing those of one Hayashi student to another. Tatsumi's symbols are slightly different to Mrs Yamaguchi's and again it seems from those received via Sensei Takeuchi in the RJKD lineage. All are different to those that the *Gakkai* are familiar with.

Also of note is the suggestion that originally Hayashi would also give four or five additional empowerments (not attunements) to his most advanced teacher-level students. These apparently formed a part of the inner teachings of the system given to him and Eguchi by Usui. It does open up speculation as to whether or not these empowerments bear any relationship to the four empowerments given in *Buddho-EnerSense* which form the basis of the inner teachings of the Reiki system as taught by Reiki Jin Kei Do, as we do know that at the very least Hayashi was aware of and passed on the *Buddho* meditation. It must be a credible speculation therefore that he was also familiar with the empowerment that went with it (the energetic 'permission' to engage in the practice).

It is possible that Hayashi and by extension, Usui, was aware of more of the *Buddho-EnerSense* system than just the first three cycles of the *Buddho* meditation. Clearly Hayashi was aware of at least some, if not the majority, of the elements or higher teachings of the spiritual development side of the system which includes the immensely powerful Vajrayana practice of the *Buddho*.

Hayashi conducted intensive training seminars all over Japan, training hundreds of students in his system of Reiki. In total however he only taught 17 Reiki Masters. One of these was the enigmatic abbot of a small Zen temple; Sensei Takeuchi. It was to Takeuchi that Hayashi passed on the *Buddho* meditation. Takeuchi, who may have been a close friend, was not considered a 'typical' student by Hayashi. Perhaps others also received the *Buddho.* Certainly Takeuchi seems to have inherited a form of Usui's system that is similar in many ways – with the exception of the *Buddho* meditation – to that which was passed on to another of Hayashi's students, Hawayo Takata, from whom the majority of the Reiki in the world is descended.

With the outbreak of World War 2 and its consequent escalating savagery, Hayashi felt a strong conflict between his impending military call-up and his moral code as a Reiki practitioner. Because he had visited Hawaii in 1938 (to promote Reiki and to complete the training of Hawayo Takata) there was a distinct possibility that he would be executed as a spy if he did not got to war, and so in the presence of some of his own students and his wife at his villa in the hot spring resort of Atami, near Mt Fuji, on 11 May 1940, he took his own life. His wife Chie continued to teach Reiki in her husband's place at the Reiki School and throughout Japan and also maintained his clinic during the 1940s, but this was not continued by their children after Chie had passed on.

## Seiji Takamori

It was the current lineage head, Dr Ranga Premaratna, who noted that the name Seiji Takamori means 'True' (*Sei*) – 'Compassion' or 'Love' (*Ji*) – 'Eagle' (*Taka*) – 'Observe' (*Mori*). Therefore his name means 'true compassion and eagle-like observation', and is an expression of the philosophical basis of Reiki Jin Kei Do, which we look at in the next chapter.

## His Early Life and Training

Seiji Takamori was born in 1907 and at the age of 19 became a Zen monk under Sensei Takeuchi. Following five years of intensive meditation instruction in the Zen tradition, Takamori was introduced to Reiki by his teacher at Takamori's request. Seiji did not study Reiki in the 3-degrees form as we now know it. A style of teaching seems to have been used that was reminiscent of Usui's approach in that training was not done over short periods of two days or so, or in weekend classes as is generally the modern Western way but as a continuing process of education and practice. Seiji seems to have learnt the system incrementally over a period of three years before finally being considered a Reiki Master and empowered to teach the system to others. His progress was regularly monitored by Takeuchi who would check the degree or intensity of Seiji's energy transmission. During this period Seiji was required to give healing to the local village residents who supported the temple.

Seiji Takamori was the only student to whom Sensei Takeuchi passed on the complete Reiki system as he knew it, including the *Buddho* meditation, which was given to him as a part of his own Masters training.

## His Quest and Beyond

Seiji was something of a pioneer and had a deep commitment to exploring the nature of human consciousness and to achieving enlightenment in his lifetime. In recognizing the Buddhist origins of the *Buddho* meditation, Seiji requested that Venerable Takeuchi allow him to search for further teachings relating to Reiki and the Buddhist material that he had been given. In receiving this permission he began a process of extensively researching the origins of the Reiki system over a period of 20 years within the Tantric and Vajrayana schools of Buddhism, which took him on a journey from Japan to northern India, Nepal and Tibet. After a few years in yogic ashrams, learning the Hindi, Sanskrit and Tibetan languages, he went up into the Himalayas to search for monks who might continue his education in meditation and healing. In an isolated part of Nepal he discovered a more complete system of healing and spiritual development that paralleled his own practice of Reiki. The order of recluse monks that he discovered knew the three cycles of the *Buddho* meditation and were familiar with various healing methods that relied upon the power of the mind. Their practice also included the use of two of the Reiki symbols and echoed the Buddhist teachings that Seiji had been given. It was clear to Seiji that there was a direct link between the philosophy and the symbols, yantras and mantras of this system and the philosophy, symbols and practices of the Reiki system. Indeed he realized that two of the Reiki symbols were in fact translations of mantras used in the *Buddho* method. It was Seiji's belief that he had discovered the same or similar material within Vajrayana Buddhism that Usui had connected to and possibly used in developing his system of *Usui Do*. The connections seemed obvious. He decided to stay and study with three of the monks. After a period of time he was directed to a more senior monk further into the mountains who knew the complete system, with whom he spent a further seven years. The system of *Buddho-EnerSense*, as it came to be known, that Seiji learnt is thought to be a parallel system of healing and spiritual development, passed down from the Buddha that relates to the origins of Reiki as developed by Usui and his students. It is possible that Usui had access to texts that may have contained information on a simple form of the *Buddho* system, along with the *Buddho* meditation itself. As a system of mind/body healing the *Buddho-EnerSense* method is unique. It is a practice that develops and refines the practitioner's awareness of and sensitivity to the energy fields of the body including the *chakras*, *nadis* and *marma* points through meditation and through a series of exercises specifically designed for this purpose. Critical to the *Buddho-EnerSense* system and thus to its simplified form in the RJKD system of Reiki is the development of compassion and wisdom and the integration of these qualities into the life of the practitioner. Reiki Master Tony Birdfield has speculated on the origins of the *Buddho* meditation in a story that goes back to the historical Buddha.

The *Buddho* meditation was given by the Buddha to the Bodhisattva Avalokiteshvara. Avalokiteshvara had made a vow to postpone his own enlightenment until all other sentient beings had become liberated and it was because of this vow of pure compassion for others that the Buddha passed on the *Buddho* meditation. This meditation was then passed from Avalokiteshvara to a monk who began to develop a complete system of meditation and healing around the *Buddho* and drawing on *Ayurvedic* medicine (*Marma Shastra*) and Indian martial arts (in which he had been trained prior to becoming a monk). This extensive mind/body healing system was then transmitted from India to Tibet by Vairochana. Vairochana was one of the 25 disciples of Padmasambhava – The Tantric Buddha. Due to political conflicts Vairochana ended up living in exile on the borders of Tibet and China and so the system, including the *Buddho* meditation, was carried from China to other parts of the Far East including Japan. As a consequence of Chinese military expansionism the system underwent further development in the hands of Theravadan monks living in exile who practiced an early form of Buddhist meditation. So the healing method which had started out as a simple but powerful meditation practice developed over time into a highly complex system and then returned to the simplicity of its origins. Ultimately the system was taken to Nepal where it was accessed by Seiji Takamori. The *Buddho-EnerSense* system therefore seems to be rooted in the Vajrayana tradition of Highest Yoga Tantra with origins in early Indian Buddhist practices (such as *Vipassana* meditation) and even earlier Hindu Yogic practices.

On completion of his studies Seiji left Nepal and travelled the world teaching meditation and healing and being supported by those requesting teachings from him. In the early part of the 1970s Seiji visited Hawaii to look for Hawayo Takata.

Hawayo Takata was the last Reiki Master trained by Hayashi and referred to her style of Reiki as *Usui Shiki Ryoho*. It is from her lineage that the majority of Reiki in the world is practised, and her teachings that have predominantly defined the system up until recent times. As a consequence of World War 2 she lost contact with Hayashi's Reiki School in which she had done much of her training, and the other Japanese practitioners, and thought herself to be the last surviving Reiki Master in the world (presumably until she met Seiji Takamori).

Seiji and Hawayo Takata met sometime during the 1970s. It is believed that in exchange for possibly meditation instruction or energy empowerments, Seiji received the Masters attunement in the Takata lineage so that he might experience the highest level of energy that she could transmit. It is important to note that Seiji was not trained by Takata and nothing of this mutual exchange of knowledge and energy informed the teachings that later became known as Reiki Jin Kei Do. Seiji was already a fully trained Reiki Master in his own right at the time of this meeting, and the mutual energy exchange that took place was simply to experience and appreciate each other's connection to Mikao Usui and Chujiro Hayashi.

After leaving the US, Seiji travelled and taught in Asia for a period of time before returning to the US in 1990 to teach meditation. It was during this period that he met Dr Ranga Premaratna in Madison, Wisconsin, where Ranga was working as a researcher. During the visit Seiji passed on the complete Reiki system that he had been taught and the researched Buddhist material that he had discovered in the Himalayas. Ranga was the only person to receive the full teachings from Seiji and with whom my own Reiki Masters, Gordon and Dorothy Bell trained.

Seiji eventually died whilst sitting in meditation at a Buddhist monastery in Sri Lanka in 1992 at the age of 83.

## Seiji's Legacy

So another lineage of Reiki emerged from Japan, a lineage with a distinctly different ethos and approach to that of the dominant Western lineages. This lineage is now known as Reiki Jin Kei Do (The Way of Compassion and Wisdom through Reiki), and contains within it the traditional 3-Degree Reiki system that came largely from Hayashi, and also the system of *Buddho-EnerSense* which is only available as further studies within this lineage. Due to the emphasis of the people who have carried the system of Reiki from the time of Hayashi however, there has been a fundamental shift back to Reiki as a spiritual development tool with the potential of leading the practitioner to their own experience of *satori*, rather than simply as a healing or complementary therapy method.

The teachings and practices of Reiki within this lineage are fundamentally rooted in and are a simplified form of the *Buddho-EnerSense* method, and connect to the Sanskrit/Tibetan origins, mantras, yantras, symbols and meditations that it is believed informed Usui's development of the *Usui Do* system. What Seiji ultimately gave to the world was a system of healing and spiritual development that it would seem, is as close in ethos to Usui's original *Usui Do* (from our current state of knowledge on the subject), as we can get at present. This of course does not preclude those systems currently being developed from what appears to be excellent and well-researched material into the actual methods that Usui employed. Whilst RJKD is very much an evolving practice in terms of its methodology, understanding and philosophy, it has not taken on board recent developments and techniques from Japanese or Western Reiki. Its approach has been to assimilate practices that reinforce its essential ethos or message, but not to incorporate every newly discovered method.

Whilst these may have value, they can sometimes be seen as only serving to confuse and provide the practitioner with more in the way of worldly attachments and distractions from the true purpose of the RJKD system.

## Ranga Premaratna

Ranga is from a Sri Lankan Buddhist background and has been familiar with the practice of meditation since the age of 15. During a period in 1978 in Hawaii when he began his degree studies in Food and Nutritional Science, he undertook some further studies in Buddhism and in complementary therapies such as reflexology, *shiatsu* and *kiatsu*. He then moved to Indiana in mainland USA to undertake a PhD but also continued with his studies in natural medicines, bodywork and meditation. In 1989 Ranga received his PhD in Food Microbiology and Biotechnology from Purdue University and was offered a job at the Food Research Institute of the University of Wisconsin as a postdoctoral research scientist. He accepted the offer, and with his wife Mae moved to the beautiful town of Madison. This proved to be a profound turning point in his life.

As he continued with his meditation practice he constantly had the feeling that there was a healing method that involved the use of the hands that was unlike anything he had come across before. Then one weekend he discovered a copy of Barbara Weber Ray's book *The Reiki Factor* in an esoteric bookshop called *Shakthi*. Ranga became intrigued by this system of Reiki and began to look for classes. He tried to contact Weber Ray, but was unsuccessful. A couple of weeks later he found himself again at the bookshop and there was a poster for a Reiki class. Ranga signed up for the class and so, in November 1989, he began his Reiki training in the Takata lineage of Western Reiki with Elka Petra Palm from West Germany, from whom he received both the 1st and 2nd Degrees. Almost a year later, after seeing another advertisement at *Shakthi* he went on to take his Masters level training with another Takata lineage teacher, Beth Sanders. Initially impressed with the energetic experience and the way that it helped with his meditation practice, Ranga developed a sense of unease about some of the material that was being presented to him, particularly in relation to the Reiki symbols that were being described by Petra Palm and Sanders as Sanskrit in origin, which clearly they were not. Nor in fact were the so-called Tibetan symbols passed on to him by Sanders as a part of his Masters training, Tibetan at all. As a consequence of the dubiousness of this material, Ranga felt that perhaps he had been too hasty in his search for a teacher and so decided to simply work with what he had, integrated with his meditation practice. He undertook a nine-day intensive meditation programme and asked to be guided to the teacher who could show him the right path, and so Ranga had begun his search for the true information on Reiki and the Reiki symbols.

A few days later, towards the end of November 1990, Ranga met Seiji Takamori after being introduced to him over the phone by a relative of his living in San Francisco, who had met the monk in a park where he was sitting in meditation. Seiji had gone to the relative's house for a meal when a phone call from Ranga interrupted them. Ranga was phoning to suggest Reiki treatments as a possible way of dealing with an illness from which this relative was suffering. Seiji overheard the conversation and the mention of the word 'Reiki'. A conversation between Seiji and Ranga followed in which Ranga managed to persuade Seiji to visit and to teach him meditation and Reiki, but no specific arrangements were made. Then one day whilst walking near a lake, Ranga heard the sound of chanting. He came upon a man with a Japanese top-knot who then got up to perform a series of exercises that were reminiscent of *Tai Chi*. Ranga described his experience of this moment:

> Each arm movement seemed to generate surges of energy that I could feel from a distance. Just watching this man move from one powerful action to the next sent shivers throughout my body.

Ranga was ultimately trained in the complete Reiki system and the older healing method on which elements of the Reiki system were based that Seiji had rediscovered in the Himalayas. The training was intensive over a relatively short period of time and included meditation practice that could go on for three or four hours at a time. The Buddhist method that Seiji passed on to Ranga was simply referred to by Seiji by the name of its key meditation practice: *Buddho*. However, following its transmission to Ranga, and in discussion with his teacher, Ranga coined the term *EnerSense* (to denote 'energy' and 'senses' or 'sensations') to appeal to non-Buddhists.

Seiji asked Ranga that he continue the work of healing and the transmission of the knowledge imparted to him to those who were ready. Seiji believed that the time was right to spread this ancient method of *Buddho* into the modern world where people would be ready to receive the knowledge of this healing system for their own benefit and to help those that would be attracted to the method as a way of life.

Following the completion of his training Ranga went on to teach this new lineage of Reiki to his old Reiki Master, Beth Sanders, who received all three levels from him, but only the basics of the *Buddho-EnerSense* system, as he was not at that point ready to teach the system in its entirety.

Upon his arrival in Australia in 1992 Ranga began to teach the new lineage on a wider basis along with the *Buddho-EnerSense* method. At first the lineage did not have a name and was referred to in numerous ways, often simply being called *The Eastern Lineage of Reiki* (As opposed to the Western – Takata – Lineage). Clearly there were other eastern lineages of Reiki, and so in 1997 Ranga gave the lineage the name *Reiki Jin Kei Do* and thus began a process of defining the specific orientation of the lineage and teachings. For a period of time the teachings of RJKD were given the name of *Usui Shin Kai* in the belief that they went to the heart of the Usui system (*Usui Shin Kai* means 'The True (or Heart/Core) Teachings of Usui). Whilst this still pertains to a degree, it has become clear from the evidence of continued research into the nature of Usui's system, that the Reiki material given to Ranga by Seiji is fundamentally enriched and impregnated by the *Buddho-EnerSense* system, and that there are clear differences between it and the newly emerging Japanese Reiki styles that also have their roots in Usui's system. The term *Usui Shin Kai* has now been dropped and Reiki Jin Kei Do is now the name given both to the lineage and to the teachings that it contains. As I have stated elsewhere however, RJKD does share a common ancestry with Takata lineage Reiki through the person of Chujiro Hayashi, and as such does reflect his approach to the system. Thus RJKD contains material relating to the use of Reiki as a therapeutic discipline; it is not regarded as a focus of the system, but merely another tool for exploring and developing an understanding of oneself through the expression of universal compassion for other beings.

During the mid to late 1990s, as the teachings of RJKD and *Buddho-EnerSense* spread, Ranga began to appoint Lineage Representatives in various parts of the globe to oversee the further dissemination of the teachings. The role of Lineage Representative has however fallen from use to some degree in recent years, but this role is currently being revived so that the Lineage Representatives can take a much more proactive role and become contact points and sources of information for all teachers and students within the lineage.

In 2005 a major review of the lineage and where it stands in relation to its own core philosophy and the mechanics of the dissemination of its teachings was initiated. This came at a time when it was felt that there was a need to 'bring together' the RJKD family as a discreet body of practitioners and Masters within the wider Reiki community for a period of self-reflection and analysis. Many aspects of the lineage, its practices and orientation to those practices have come under review, and are discussed further in Chapter 12.

✳

The Lineage of Reiki Jin Kei Do does not contain channelled material, but does incorporate practice and philosophy from various other sources, such as *Qi Gong*, Buddhist meditation, *Ayurvedic Marma Point* theory, and classical Chinese medical philosophy. It also includes much theory and practice around the functions of the *chakras* and *nadis*. Whether the energetic system of the body was ever a part of Usui's system or not, it is a part of the RJKD system as Seiji, seeing the practice of Reiki from the perspective of the *Buddho-EnerSense* method, considered this to be important. This drawing on various sources is very much in keeping with the method that Usui employed in developing his system in the first instance. Thus RJKD is a discreet and coherent practice that needs no other extraneous material to 'improve' it or to update it.  Whilst teachers of the lineage may also teach from other Reiki lineages and branches, none of this material is presented as a part of the RJKD teachings that continue to be passed on from one teacher to the next in their whole form. This is not to say that RJKD teachers will not include other practices within the class context, but all will provide a minimum of the Core Teachings with possibly extra material that fits in with the overall philosophic aims of the lineage.

## Some Thoughts on Lineage

The common currency of lineage in Reiki is a subject that is often brushed over or even dismissed in a very negative way by those who fail to understand the importance of this tradition for the passing on of spiritual teachings that gather within their ambit the knowledge and wisdom of those who have gone before. Reiki Masters and practitioners often proclaim that they come from this or that lineage, but how often do they stop to think about what this really means to them and their practice and their role as representatives of a particular lineage? What is it that is meant by lineage and why is it so important?

Lineage is often talked about in terms of personalities. In

the case of this particular lineage, we can say that it starts with Mikao Usui and carries on down to the current lineage head, Dr Ranga Premaratna and then on to all of the other Masters and practitioners within the tradition, but this is really only a small part of how we should define lineage. Lineage is not just about the personalities, but most importantly it is about the vessel that they carry. Indeed, the vessel is the lineage. We define a lineage for ease through the naming of key people who have carried it for us or made a significant contribution to it. Individuals may at times put something extra into the lineage vessel, or even take something out, but this is done with a sense of awareness of what is and what is not appropriate at any given moment or in any given situation – the sum of this process being to enhance that which they already hold, and thus have something of increased value to pass on to others. Thus wisdom is accumulated. These people serve as protectors of the teachings as indeed we all do as representatives of a lineage but with a sense of awareness of the love and compassion that has gone into not only the forging of the vessel, but also the distilling of universal truths by our spiritual forebears and contemporaries that add to the sum total of the teachings; the contents of the vessel. To be a part of a lineage is to accept the responsibility in helping to shoulder the sacred load and carry it for future students and subsequent generations to access for the ultimate betterment of all humankind. This is a big undertaking, and needs to be approached with a sense of the sacred and with a deep commitment to being the living embodiment of the teachings. This is not to say that we must never falter and are not allowed to make mistakes on our journey through life, but we do need to recognize our failings and treat ourselves with the compassion and forgiveness that will ultimately set an example for others to follow.

The lineage vessel is however also very much empowered by and in part defined by the energetic matrix that is built around it and through it by the vibrational qualities of the personalities who have carried it. When we talk about a lineage as a line of people what we are really talking about is our energetic connection to them, passed on via the attunement process, which remains as a permanent part of our own energy profile. Many people involved in the practice of Reiki may have experienced this energetic connection to their line of teachers for themselves. This may be as a student receiving the attunement, or as a teacher in giving the attunement. This connection can be quite palpable and feel, certainly for me whilst giving an attunement, as if my lineage – those that have carried the vessel down to me – are all in the room with me. This is a very special and often quite profound feeling of connectivity to a stream of pure energy that gives the lineage its own unique 'flavor'.

What it means to become a part of a lineage was beautifully described by Jack Kornfield in his book *A Path with Heart:*

> ...as we select a teacher, we join a tradition and lineage as well. Lineages are the carriers of ancient wisdom. In every great tradition, the shamans, the healers, the yogis, the wise women of the mystery schools, the great rabbis or desert fathers, live within their lineage. Lineage and tradition are the sacred containers for preserving practices and wisdom that have been discovered and accumulated over generations. Lineages are the form through which the light of awakening is passed from one generation to the next.
>
> When we choose a teacher, we are drawn into the powerful current of a lineage and partake of its worldview, its visions, its possibilities, and its limitations. Every lineage and tradition has both possibilities and limitations. In the wisest traditions, the higher teachings will guide its members to recognize and transcend the very limitations of the tradition's own form, to discover the sacred that is within themselves beyond all form.
>
> The choosing of a lineage or set of practices, like choosing a teacher, is a mysterious process in which we are drawn or attracted to a spiritual stream. Again, trust yourself, and look for integrity, joy and maturity in the community.

# My Lineage

Mikao Usui
Chujiro Hayashi
Sensei Takeuchi
Seiji Takamori
Ranga Premaratna
Gordon and Dorothy Bell
Steve Gooch

# 5

# The Philosophy of RJKD

Compassion is the ultimate and most meaningful
embodiment of emotional maturity. It is through
compassion that a person achieves the highest peak
and deepest reach in his or her search for self-
fulfillment.

*Arthur Jersild*

In an interview with Tony Birdfield in 2003, the lineage head,
Dr. Ranga Premaratna, described the essential purpose of both
the Reiki and *Buddho-EnerSense* systems in this way:

> ...the fundamental goals of both systems are...to move
> towards an enlightened state of mind; a mind that is not
> hindered by conditioned patterns that we have created over
> many lifetimes or even within this life.

The name Reiki Jin Kei Do was coined by Ranga in an effort
to more precisely define what it is that the lineage stands for,

and to encapsulate the essence of the teachings which it contains. Through its common heritage via Hayashi it has many similarities with the Takata lineage style of Reiki, but there are also many distinct differences, and the naming of the lineage has helped to clarify the position on the RJKD practice of Reiki. Most importantly the name reflects the fundamental philosophy of the teachings. To understand this philosophy we need to break the name down into its component parts and examine what these mean.

*Jin* is the Japanese word for 'compassion' and represents the Buddhist concept of universal compassion for all beings. This is known as *karuna* in Sanskrit and is one of the products or fruits of deep and committed spiritual training.

*Kei* is the Japanese for 'wisdom'. This represents the Buddhist understanding of universal wisdom and again is the product of deep spiritual practice. This concept of wisdom is known as *prajna* in Sanskrit.

*Do* is the Japanese for 'way' or 'path' (translated as *Tao* in Chinese). This links the concepts of compassion and wisdom with the healing aspects of Reiki, so that Reiki is seen as a path of spiritual development that integrates healing with sustained meditation practice. It is a path or a way of life that is lead through the expression and natural outflow of universal compassion and wisdom, and thus healing, in a balanced way.

Healing is one of the important qualities of the application of Reiki in RJKD. By emphasizing the practice of self-treatment with a feeling of compassion for oneself and by developing awareness of the energy flow through focusing on the upper four *chakras* and palms (meditating with the hands) we begin to generate the quality of unconditional love for ourselves. This is an essential, even critical part of the healing process. As we continue to work with Reiki, the feelings of compassion that we have begun to develop for ourselves are enhanced even further. This is accompanied by the development of a sensation of warmth and expansiveness in the heart due to the Reiki energy expanding and opening the heart center and so enabling us to completely fill ourselves with this energy of compassion. As this feeling grows it then allows for the opportunity to extend the feeling of love and universal compassion to others through our practice of Reiki. The flow of Reiki is enhanced or magnified significantly by this feeling of compassion in our own heart. Of course Reiki will flow in any case, but this can so often be a cold and dispassionate process, and ultimately devoid of any warmth and notions of caring for the recipient. In this case Reiki becomes more like an obligation, or a way of making a living than a hand extended in love. We need to empower our Reiki hands with compassion from the heart.

Meditation and the consequent development of wisdom is another important aspect of the practice within RJKD. Following the 1st Degree attunements, basic instructions in a simple meditation method are provided. This meditation is to enable students to develop awareness to the Reiki energy flow in their bodies and through the *chakra* and *nadi* system. During the process of meditation, as the mind enters deeper states, the vibrational frequencies increase dramatically. As a student progresses through the levels of training they are given further instructions and guidance to help them increase their sensitivity to this flow and to become aware of the way in which the energy constantly fluctuates in the physical body. This process is enhanced by the introduction of the inherently powerful Reiki symbols, which amplify the energy further. As the student develops their sense of awareness they begin to see how thoughts constantly arise and pass away in a rapid and ceaseless succession. The mind's ability to clearly see the changing thought process is promoted by its increasing awareness of and sensitivity to the energy flux. This ultimately leads to the development of insight and wisdom.

Eventually, with the regular practice of meditation, particularly when the Reiki symbols are incorporated, it is possible to realize non-self, non-duality. This is the ultimate realization of our energetic state of oneness with the Universal Energy Field or God. As we achieve this state our ego-centeredness is melted away as we lose our sense of being an individual entity, and so we begin to see and recognize ourselves in every being. It is simply a shift in our mind's awareness. This recognition of our commonality with every other being promotes a feeling of universal compassion and a deep and profound wisdom into the nature of everything, and it is at this point that we can become truly free of all that has shackled us throughout our lives.

The path of RJKD is one of integrating the wisdom mind of

meditation with the compassion of Reiki and making this one's way of life and this is ultimately the path to enlightenment.

## Compassion

It is important to understand what it is that is meant by 'compassion' as there is often much confusion around this seemingly simple word and concept.

It might be helpful to look at the Chinese word for compassion: *ci bei*. The first character *ci* translates as *maitri* in Sanskrit, which means 'to give happiness'. The second, *bei* (*karuna* in Sanskrit) means 'to remove suffering'. Together they show that the feeling of compassion is the activity or function of relieving living beings of suffering (or *duhkha* in Sanskrit) and giving them happiness. To have compassion is to be engaged in an active and dynamic process. It is not merely an expression of 'sympathy' for someone's lot. Sympathy implies a hierarchical structure where the sympathetic person sees themselves as somehow better or better off than the person who is the focus of the sympathy and is entirely devoid of any real understanding of the nature of the person's suffering. Sympathy is entirely outward looking, and not generated from a heart of true understanding that we are all equal in our sufferings, though each may have a different flavor from person to person. Sympathy is also bereft of action. Sympathy is generated from the head, whilst compassion comes from the heart. Sympathy must become a generator first of empathy and then of true heart-felt compassion. Compassion is a dynamic, powerful and infinitely sublime motive force that by its very nature changes the perceived reality of the recipient and that of the person generating the compassion, and the two become one, even just for a moment.

We all have problems, some of which we can solve for ourselves, and for some of which we need the help of others. We all from time to time need the kindness of someone else to get us through a bad patch, or to support us in some way.

It is easy to be kind to someone who has shown us kindness, but the spirit of true compassion requires of us that we be kind towards all people, even to those that we are indifferent to or might not like very much because they have done us some wrong. This is, without fail, one of the hardest challenges for anyone, but to realize true freedom and a full expression of the heart it is a path that we must take. This is the path of the Bodhisattva. It is a true and often repeated statement that our worst enemies are in fact our best friends as they can teach us so much. The most important thing that they can teach us is to let go of our ego-centered feelings of hurt, pain, fear or anger and understand that the other person too is suffering and for this reason are an ideal recipient of our compassion. As Nichiren Daishonin wrote: "Even a heartless villain loves his wife and children. He too has a portion of the Bodhisattva world within him." He too is connected to the power of the Universal Energy Field and is one with it. True compassion requires courage and strength.

Kindness that does not empower the receiver creates little lasting value. Real compassion is that which has the power to root out the cause of misery and direct people to the cause of happiness. It is in this sense that Reiki can be seen as a powerful method of embodying and conveying compassion for others as by its very nature it promotes a sense of wellbeing and ultimately happiness.

Compassion must start with oneself however. We are all prone to seeing problems in the world around us, to see suffering and injustice and want to do something about it. Sometimes what we see in the world around us can cause us to become angry or outraged and we rally against the perceived object of our anger in an effort to reform it, to make it better, to solve the injustice or ease the suffering. What we need to realize is that the problem is firstly inside of us. It is the way that we perceive and relate to the problems of the world or the suffering of another that is the real problem. Once we work on ourselves, and realize that we too have problems and are in need of compassion, that we too are not always in the right and can make mistakes and that we need to forgive ourselves and see ourselves as the rightful recipients of love and understanding, then we can truly begin to empathize with the suffering of others. We can put ourselves in their shoes. In this spirit of true understanding we can then offer active compassion in a way that will not only relieve the person's suffering but also promote a sense of wellbeing and happiness. We are all equal in our need for compassion and love.

Forgiveness is often a necessary first step before we can feel or generate compassion. When someone has hurt us deeply, particularly if it is someone close to us, it is hard to offer compassion for the suffering that they might be experiencing. We can feel angry and resentful because they have taken away our happiness. But this anger and resentment may be hiding the true nature of our pain as we project it outwards. The first step in this is to look with honesty inside ourselves and acknowledge whatever we find there that might have contributed in some way to the hurt that was inflicted on us. What is it that we did to provoke or manifest the painful experience? In what way was our energetic resonance a match with that of the other person to 'pull in' this painful experience? There will be something! It is only when we can acknowledge our own role in this type of situation that we can begin to effect real healing. Firstly we must forgive ourselves, truly and deeply for our own role in the mutual hurt. Once we can do this, then there is room for an understanding of the actions and motives of the other, and we can then begin to forgive them too. As a consequence of this process of forgiveness, we can sincerely empathize with the true nature of their suffering as it is a mirror of our own, and thus we have sown the seeds of real compassion and mutual understanding. Ultimately, we simply have to let go of the emotion and just *be* compassion. As the saying goes: the sun does not stop shining just because there are clouds in the sky.

I was watching a TV news report some years ago about a group of animal rights activists campaigning to stop the transport of veal calves across Europe. The camera dwelt for a while on an outraged protestor, who having managed to corner one of the people from the company that was involved in the trade, launched into a quite shocking tirade of verbal abuse and personal character assassination of the company representative. No matter the rightness or wrongfulness of the morality of the issue, this protestor, in failing to see that her own anger and expression of violent outrage was no better than the physical violence reportedly conducted by the transport company, did a huge amount of damage to her cause. This is a good example of how the little self, the ego, can hijack the idea of compassion, because there is no real understanding of it, and use it for its own ends; as a weapon. We do not know the reality of the company representative. We do not know why he was in the situation of being in that particular line of work. Perhaps, for reasons unknown to us and the protestor, he had little or no choice. He had his path through life and there is a need to not only respect it, but honor it and love him for it. This is not to say that we must turn a blind eye to injustice or violence in the world, but that we should approach it with love and an open heart and with a deep sense of knowing. How are we contributing to the pain and suffering in the world? The protestor in her profound sense of empathy for the suffering of those animals allowed herself to also become hurt, and then tried to lash out at the perceived cause of the hurt. This of course did not make hers or the animals' pain go away; it simply increased the pain in the world by inflicting hurt on the company representative. Whatever we do with our lives, we and everyone else are constantly generating the need for compassion. In working inwards in the first instance, it is easy to see the truth of the fact that others as well as ourselves desperately need this compassion. This includes everyone – all beings, not just cuddly animals seen through misty eyes.

Jack Kornfield in *A Path with Heart* noted:

> Compassionate generosity is the foundation of true spiritual
> life because it is the practice of letting go. An act of generosity

opens our body, heart, and spirit and brings us closer to freedom. Each act of generosity is a recognition of our interdependence, an expression of our Buddha nature.

## Wisdom

It is the development and gaining of wisdom (*prajna*) and insight into the nature of all things that enables us to connect fully with our heart of compassion. This wisdom is described within the Buddhist Eightfold Path, when it says that the gaining of a 'right view' is when we have a true understanding of The Four Noble Truths and we have the aspiration or strong desire to free ourselves from attachment, ignorance and hatefulness. The Four Noble Truths are that (a) life is full of suffering (b) this suffering is due to attachment or desire (c) we can overcome attachment and desire (d) there is a way or method for doing this.

As he sat at the foot of the banyan tree by the banks of the Neranjara River, the following thought arose in the mind of the Buddha:

> This is the only way that leads to the attainment of purity, to the overcoming of sorrow and lamentation, to the end of pain and grief, to the entering of the right path and to the realization of Nibbana (Nirvana): this way is the Four Foundations of Mindfulness.

According to the Buddha we need to contemplate the Four Noble Truths in order to purify the mind. If we can fully realize the reality of these Four Noble Truths then our minds will be purified and enlightened, and this will lead to the extinction of suffering – the attainment of *Nibbana* (which is the state of being that follows from the total annihilation of the round of suffering).

The understanding that life is full of suffering and that this is due to our attachments to things, people, circumstances, memories, emotions and everything else in our sphere of human existence is due to our mistaken efforts at permanence. We keep clinging to things, each other and ourselves in a fruitless effort to achieve this state of permanence. We strive for a permanent state of health, or financial security, or love, or good looks, or life, but the world is imperfect, impermanent and not separate from us. Our limited view of what we believe to be reality however suggests that we are separate, and that we can achieve a state happiness through things, or people, or the generating of certain emotions, but none of these last, and so the cycle of grasping, craving and clinging in a selfish way starts all over again.

Once we realize that this is a never-ending cycle of pain, we can begin to develop the desire to free ourselves from it. We can begin to see that it is our attachments that weigh us down through life, and it is our ignorance of the true state of being that keeps us bound to these attachments and that this binding is of our own making and so can only be broken by ourselves.

Through our meditation practice we ultimately come to acknowledge that not only is there a pure state of non-duality, but even on a mundane level we can recognize our interdependence. We sit on chairs made by other people and eat food cooked by other people from ingredients grown by others. Our clothes are made by other people. As much as we would like to think that we achieve our successes in life simply through our own efforts with no recourse to anyone else our lives are in fact intrinsically interwoven with everyone else and their wellbeing. We are all linked in this journey through life. As we become more and more aware of this interdependence with all other beings and the process of life itself we begin to develop a sense of responsibility for others and this ultimately leads to the giving up of selfishness and a desire to help our fellow human beings by giving back some of what we have benefited from. We start to loosen our attachments.

This is very easy to say, and is certainly easy to understand intellectually, but to truly and deeply grasp at a 'felt' level the concept that life is a never-ending cycle of attachment-based suffering that can be broken and that it is within our power to do so, is not so easy. Even harder is to know where to begin to put it into practice. Again we can look to the Buddha's Eightfold Path for the answer, and this is through 'right mindfulness' and 'right concentration'.

Both right mindfulness and right concentration are concepts that are contained within the philosophical framework of RJKD. Right mindfulness simply describes the process of focusing your attention on your body, feelings, thoughts and consciousness in such a way as to break our attachments and thus to overcome craving, ignorance and hatred. Right concentration is the effort of meditating in a way that will lead you to a progressive realization of the nature of imperfection, impermanence and non-separateness. The two concepts are fundamentally interlinked and are joined by a third: right effort. Right effort essentially enjoins us to not only gain the knowledge of the fleeting nature of all things from the practice of right mindfulness and right concentration but to use it proactively to develop our good qualities and abandon our bad qualities and thus ease our own suffering which is based on the way that we perceive reality. As we begin our practice of meditation (right concentration) we develop our skills in right mindfulness, and it is through right effort that this process of inner discovery is maintained as we use the knowledge that we have gained to improve our lives and so ease our passage through the realm of material existence. We begin to tread more lightly.

Wisdom is not something that we can find outside of ourselves. We can't buy it and we can't be given it. No matter how long we study at the feet of the wisest in the land, we can never attain wisdom for ourselves through an intellectual process. It is innate within us, but because we spend so much time engaging with the outside world and being wrapped up in our own emotional states, we build up walls or layers that stop us from accessing our own profound wisdom mind. We forget to step back from ourselves before we act or speak and so we continue the cycle of suffering by not implementing that deep inner knowing of the way to freedom. It is through the process of meditation that we begin to re-orientate ourselves and begin the process of looking inwards to see what kind of a person we truly are and to raise into consciousness the qualities of our own wisdom mind. We need to discover this wisdom and understand it for ourselves.

Compassion and wisdom are interwoven threads within the same garment. Wisdom comes from our intellectual or comprehending side of our nature, whilst compassion comes from our emotional or feeling side. When we wear this garment, we achieve a state of happiness and serenity that cannot be broken or dented by the 'slings and arrows' of the world around us. As our practice of meditation continues and we loosen the ties that bind us to the illusion of duality, separation and dependence, we begin to see not only the impermanent nature of all things, and the fact that nothing impermanent can give us permanent happiness, but also that we are truly interdependent with all other beings and that as we suffer so do they. Ranga Premaratna has noted:

> ...through observation of our own mind and body, insight wisdom arises. Simultaneously, with the understanding of the nature of reality within ourselves as well as the external world, the interdependent and inter-connected nature of our being becomes clear. With that realization one's heart opens with unconditional love or true Compassion to all beings.

The process that Ranga is describing automatically gives rise to compassion, which when suffused with wisdom enables us to let go of notions of how things 'should be' and what is 'right' for any situation or person. Without wisdom, compassion will not work. Wisdom allows us to be unconditioned and unbiased in our expression of compassion. So we let go of what we think is right so that we can clearly see what is actually helpful.

It is the qualities of compassion and wisdom that we try to develop through the practice of the teachings contained within

RJKD. These are essentially the tools of our trade that we hone in our efforts to try to achieve a state of healing and harmony through the easing of suffering for all, including ourselves. Through applying our gifts as channels for Reiki we can bring to bear the loving nature of the universe as an expression of our compassion and wisdom in a direct and powerful way to ease suffering in the world and to effect healing. As our compassion grows and we search for methods to help others on their journey through life, we are naturally drawn to the channeling of Reiki (the energy of compassion) as a profound gift of healing that has within it an essential wisdom which we endeavor through our efforts in meditation to attune ourselves too. In harmonizing our hearts of compassion and our minds of wisdom we become powerful generators of Reiki and thus are able to open the door to the infinite for others to walk through. In this way, healing is the beginning of the journey back to the discovery of our true nature as perfect and unconditioned – one with the All. The Buddha:

On life's journey
Faith is nourishment,
Virtuous deeds are a shelter,
Wisdom is the light by day and
Right mindfulness is the protection by night.
If a man lives a pure life nothing can destroy him;
If he has conquered greed nothing can limit his freedom.

# 6

# The Three Degrees
of Reiki

Only if one knows the truth of love, which is the real
nature of Self, will the strong entangled knot of life
be untied. Only if one attains the height of love will
liberation be attained. The experience of Self is only
love, which is seeing only love, hearing only love,
feeling only love, tasting only love and smelling only
love, which is bliss.

*Ramana Maharishi*

In bringing students to develop their innate qualities of
compassion and wisdom and to set them on the road to which
the ultimate goal is freedom or enlightenment, the lineage
teachings focus on a series of practices and principles. These are
based on those that Sensei Takeuchi received from Hayashi but
were developed further by Takamori and Premaratna and are
thus very different to those of the Takata lineage. The system of
Reiki that continued from Takeuchi is what we know as Reiki Jin
Kei Do. Within this tradition of Reiki there is an emphasis on a

more meditative approach. It is an orientation of Reiki that began with Usui but with the contribution of Seiji Takamori developed into a new form – Reiki Jin Kei Do. The teachings within this form that began with Usui, Hayashi, Takeuchi and Takamori are broadly known as Jin Kei Do to identify the orientation of the teachings and to signify the teaching style and qualities imparted by the teachers of this lineage. Within the teachings are a number of methods that underpin our practice as Reiki channels and are designed to enhance these abilities and capitalize on the potential within the Reiki system to bring healing to ourselves and others. The approach and all of the methods contained within RJKD are those that were either passed down to us from Mikao Usui, Chujiro Hayashi, Sensei Takeuchi and Seiji Takamori, or are later extrapolations of their teachings, methods and philosophy. Much material is derived from the larger teaching of *Buddho-EnerSense*. There is no claim that the methods employed are precisely the same as those taught by Usui, but the objectives and the potentiality of the teachings delivers us to the essence of the Usui system.

As with the Takata lineages, in RJKD the system of Reiki is broken down into three distinct levels or degrees. Regardless of the historical origins of this division of the practice it is a format that is conducive to the teaching of weekend classes for people in the modern world whose ability to commit protracted periods of time to study is generally curtailed by the pressures of our modern societies. It is the norm for teachers of RJKD as with other teachers of Reiki to teach the system over weekends, but this is not to say that other approaches aren't equally valid. The format of the classes is entirely at the discretion of the teacher. Within each of the 1st and 2nd Degree classes there is enough material to fill a whole weekend. At 3rd Degree, the training is taken over a sustained period of time – perhaps a year or more. My own training at this level, from receiving the Masters attunement to being able to attune further Masters myself took two years of study and practice, within which was a requirement to teach the 1st and 2nd Degrees for one year prior to being allowed to initiate new Masters. Each RJKD Master will of course approach the material in their own way, and teach according to a style that suits them best, but for all there is a sense of wanting to maintain the integrity of the lineage through providing students with a thorough and well grounded knowledge of the system, its philosophy and teachings. This requires time as the student matures through the gaining of this knowledge and practical experience. The length of time taken to progress from 1st Degree through to the completion of 3rd Degree could be as short as a year or as long as ten years. The critical factor is the student's willingness to engage with the practice fully and any previous experience that they might have of energy work and meditation. As Ranga has pointed out, however, "Receiving the master level attunement and attaining mastery are two different things. Once the master level training is finished, it may take a very long time for some to attain mastery."

It is becoming increasingly common, as it appears to be within some other traditions of Reiki and with independent Reiki Masters, to teach the 3rd Degree either as a cohesive whole or to split it in to two parts, depending on the needs and desires of the student. This is my approach. There is a great deal of material available within the 3rd Degree that can benefit those students who may simply want the extra tools and increased facility given by the Masters attunement to work on themselves. Not everyone wants to go on to become a Reiki teacher. To this end, much material within this level can be taught to these students in a 3A class. 3B then follows for those who ultimately wish to go on to teach the system to others. Whichever approach is used the time frames for training largely remain the same.

Each level of training within RJKD is complete in and of itself. There is no prerequisite for the commencement of training but each level is a prerequisite for the next.

The length of the attunement process is a factor in the size of a RJKD class. Teaching one-to-one is common, but within the modern weekend class format a full compliment of students would stretch possibly to five individuals, but four would be a comfortable number in which to allow adequate time for the attunements to be performed properly. This is not to say that other approaches are not valid, and Masters have from time to time tried various approaches to accommodate larger class sizes. Given the length of time required for the Masters attunement this is generally done one-to-one outside of the context of the formal class structure, so in theory there is no limit to the size of a 3rd Degree class. Again, each RJKD teacher will approach the organization of their classes in their own way, though some guidelines are laid down for us.

Since Seiji passed on the lineage teachings to Ranga which were then disseminated across the globe, individual teachers have gone their own way in terms of their teaching styles, particular emphasis within the practice, and indeed the weight that might be given to the relevance or importance of specific techniques. The defining characteristic of the lineage is its ethos or philosophy and teachers will then decide for themselves how they realize that primary goal. What is described below is very much based on the training that I received and now pass on to my students. Not all RJKD teachers will work this way and in its modern form the lineage has many different flavors, which reflect the variety of emphases given to it by the plethora of different approaches. Consequently there will be a great deal of variety in what is presented within the Core Teachings. Recent developments within the lineage as described previously may well bring much more cohesion to the way the teachings are passed on. The important thing is not so much the detail of the components of the teachings, but the spirit or aims of the practice. The skilful means employed to realize the aims varies to a degree from one teacher to another, though all should teach as a bare minimum the established Core Teachings. However, in broad outline what follows should give you a feel for the depth and expansiveness of the teachings that make up the RJKD practice.

# 1st Degree

The 1st Degree or foundation level is structured simply and taught in the way that Seiji Takamori was taught and the way that he later taught. Students receive the attunements appropriate for this level and are provided with an introduction to what Reiki is and its evolution from the time of Usui through to the modern form of Reiki Jin Kei Do.

At this introductory level, as one would expect, many issues arise over the nature of Reiki energy, how it heals and how it can be used. Coupled with an exploration of metaphysical mind/body relationships, this is explored in depth during the 1st Degree class.

The practice of meditation is introduced at this level. Some students may well be familiar with meditation before they arrive at the class, but to realize their full potential within their practice of Reiki it is important that all learn to increase their sensitivity to the Reiki flow. To this end students are encouraged and given guidance in the practice of a simple energy awareness meditation called *The Six Point Meditation*. This is also sometimes referred to as *The Six Point Samatha Meditation* — *Samatha* meaning 'tranquillity' or 'concentration', though *The Six Point Meditation* is in fact also used as a *Vipassana* practice. *Vipassana* can be translated as insight or mindfulness meditation and in its most basic form is designed to bring a clear awareness to the movement of both the mind and body. As the Reiki attunements sensitize us to energy flow, it is therefore possible to use *The Six Point Meditation* as a form of *Vipassana* practice as we are able to observe with clarity the movement of energy through the various channels and energy centers within the body. *The Six Point Meditation* is a much-simplified version of the *Buddho* meditation taught within the *Buddho-EnerSense* system. Students are also given a further basic *Vipassana* meditation/technique called *MindCheck*. *MindCheck* is designed to enable students to observe the movement of their minds and thus the arising of different mental states during their day.

*Metta Bhavana* or 'Loving Kindness' meditation is introduced at this level, and strikes right at the heart of the philosophy of the lineage. It is a well-known meditation practice from the Buddhist canon and provides the student with the opportunity to realize one of the basic tenets of the lineage teachings – the expressing of love and compassion first for oneself and then for all other beings. We shall look more closely at the subject of meditation in a later chapter.

The Reiki Principles, explored more fully in the next chapter, are introduced at this level. They are interpreted in a somewhat different form to the extant interpretations of other Reiki traditions, and some time is given over to looking at how these principles can be applied in our daily lives and the impact that this can have for our overall spiritual development.

Students are also taught a basic self-treatment protocol for working on the body, *chakras* and aura. The importance of this for bringing about a lasting state of physical, mental and spiritual health and harmony is emphasized, and students are advised and encouraged to include this self treatment into their daily routines and this continues through all levels of training. Treatment of others in a seated position is also taught. This is regarded as a traditional approach and is used unless the recipient is too ill or has difficulty in sitting down and then a prone position would be appropriate – maybe using a massage table. The prone position approach marks the lineage link, in common with Takata Reiki back to Dr Hayashi, as this is the way that he taught, thus students are familiarized with the practice of Reiki within other lineages. In both the seated and prone treatments students are given hand positions to work with and detailed information on the energetic nature of the specific areas of the body that relate to these hand positions. Hand positions can either be placed directly on the body or with movement in the auric field to access the various layers and sense the different fields of activity. These hand positions are very much seen as a foundation practice and not as a rigid code that always must be adhered to. As the student develops and their intuition becomes more inclined towards the sensing of these gentle fluctuations and movements within the energetic nature of the recipient, they can develop their own approach that can then use the foundation protocol as a scaffold for their own treatment structure. As students engage in treatment, whether of themselves or others, they have one more tool that they are encouraged to use, and this is the application of *The Six Point Meditation* during the period of the Reiki treatment. Thus the process of giving a treatment becomes a 'meditation with the hands'. The same approach is used as for the more formal method of engaging in this meditation, but now the energy flux is observed during the process of treatment. There are many benefits to be had from this practice, which will be discussed in the chapter on meditation.

There is one further method that is passed on to students at the 1st Degree level and that is a practice derived from *Qi Gong*, but which has a strong resonance with practices taught within the *Buddho-EnerSense* system. This is called *The Seven Purifying and Strengthening Breaths*. It is a form of standing meditation that consists of a series of movements of the arms and hands that are synchronized with the breath and thus the passage of universal energy through the body. This practice is designed to bring an awareness of energy flow through the various parts of the body, the *nadis* and *chakras*. It also helps the student to connect with the practice of mindfulness meditation, as it requires the focus with keen awareness on the flow of energy to the exclusion of external factors or influences. My personal experience of this practice is that it is a bit like having an 'energy shower'. It is incredibly empowering and uplifting but also very grounding and is ideal to do following any of the formal meditations. One student of mine indicated that he was familiar with the practice in a slightly different form and with a different emphasis from his training in *Karate*.

At the 1st Degree, students can feel overwhelmed by the plethora of new methods and philosophies as well as with coming to terms with their ability to channel Reiki. I always make it clear to my students therefore that they should not do as I first did following my 1st Degree class and that is to engage in a practice which I call 'self-flagellation by Reiki'! As a consequence of the uplifting nature of the Reiki class and the abilities imparted, it is easy to commit to the practice and methods – all of them at once – with gusto and enthusiasm and a passionate desire to get the most from the system as quickly as possible. Reiki doesn't work like this. It is necessary to be gentle with oneself, take some time, do the self-treatments and pick up the other tools when it feels right. This way, the innate intelligence of Reiki can guide you carefully and slowly through the system and lead you to a state of peace and harmony, rather than a state of stress and frustration due to having maybe missed a morning meditation. It helps to encourage students to keep a journal of their experiences with Reiki as this provides a useful tool for charting their progress and for later reflection as well as to guide their practice for the future.

## 2nd Degree

The 2nd Degree class, taken when a reasonable period of time has elapsed after the 1st Degree (about three months would be the norm), builds on the work already done. The 2nd Degree attunements are given and these work to further raise the vibrational frequencies of the Crown and Third Eye *chakras* and to empower the palm *chakras* to receive the three sacred symbols given at this level. Some time is given over to exploring the nature of the symbols and their associated mantras along with in-depth instructions on how to use them for empowering oneself and others, performing distant healing, their use in self healing and to provide mental and emotional healing. The use of the symbols and mantras as tools for personal spiritual development is also dealt with. Mindful of the fact that Reiki symbols are apt to change their visual form over time as they are passed down from one teacher to the next, all students are provided with copies of properly drawn symbols and are encouraged to learn how to draw them accurately for themselves. In this way continuity of accuracy can be maintained for future generations of students. Practice of the mantras is also important and time is given over to this. Mantra practice is a very sacred and profoundly empowering vehicle for the assimilation of spiritual qualities and attributes and it is within this spirit that the use of the Reiki mantras is developed.

2nd Degree presents a great opportunity for students to review the basic philosophy of RJKD and to report back on their progress and feelings about their practice of the 1st Degree. It is the philosophy of RJKD that ultimately underpins the practices, and for this reason it is essential to keep returning to it and to review progress in achieving its aims.

Meditation practice is further strengthened at this level. All approaches taught at the 1st Degree are developed further and may include the introduction of the Reiki symbols and mantras into the meditation, which has an incredibly empowering effect on the quality of the meditation experience and the benefits received from the practice. Within my training at this level I was also given meditations on the symbols themselves along with repetition of the associated mantras. This approach to symbol/ mantra meditation may not be consistent and widely used amongst all teachers of RJKD but is a logical extrapolation of practices within *Buddho-EnerSense*. Working with mantra in this way, as is done in some schools of Japanese Reiki, is thought to connect the practitioner to different qualities and properties of the Universal Energy Field. Students may also be shown methods of meditating on the symbols when projected onto and through the body and its energy system, and asked to sit in contemplation of the hidden meaning of the symbols. Thus at 2nd Degree, not only is the student's ability to channel energy enhanced by the attunements and the introduction of the symbols/mantras, but their progress with meditation is also potentially accelerated considerably – depending on the commitment given over to this by the student. The symbols and mantras can also be introduced into the practice of *The Seven Purifying and Strengthening Breaths*. This is probably not a common practice amongst all of the lineage teachers. I was taught this by Gordon and Dorothy who developed this (others may also have done) and introduced it into their class as a logical development of Reiki practice as seen from the point of view of someone involved with the *Buddho-EnerSense* system.

One further simple practice is introduced at this level and it is a basic energy awareness/palm activation exercise using the symbols/mantras, designed to help students really connect with the quality of energy felt between their hands and as it travels through the body/*chakras* in conjunction with the breath. It also enhances their practice of mindfulness as their full concentration is brought to bear on the flow of energy through the physical and subtle bodies.

At this level, treatment of self and others begins to depart somewhat from the Hayashi/Takata model. Both the self-treatment and seated treatment protocols change their form and are those that Seiji Takamori practised and passed on to Ranga Premaratna. Seiji worked closely with the original yogic *chakra* system and it is this, both on the body and in the aura that the hand positions focus on. It is of course customary to be able to give a treatment in the prone position also and there are two possible approaches to this. The first of these was developed by Gordon Bell at the very end of my own 2nd Degree class, and so it is probably not a common RJKD practice, though others may well have discovered this approach for themselves. By a process of extrapolation it is possible to transfer the hand positions used in the self-treatment to others whilst lying on a massage bed. This is a very powerful process, and on many occasions clients have commented to me that this way of working seems to be much more effective than the protocol used at 1st Degree. The main method of treating others in the prone position however is through the application of a treatment style introduced to the lineage by Ranga and is a 20-step full body treatment focusing on a number of specific energy points – or *marma* points (the *Ayurvedic* equivalent of the acupressure points from Traditional Chinese Medicine) – and is combined with a continued reference to the *chakra* and *nadi* system. My own experience of using this method is that clients without fail find this approach to be an incredibly powerful healing experience, so much so that I now find it inconceivable to approach treatment without drawing on elements of this method. It is interesting to note that as research into the history of Reiki progresses there seems to be more and more of a consensus that Mikao Usui may have used this or a similar methodology himself.

The 2nd Degree is considered to be the level at which students can if they desire go on to practice Reiki Therapeutics as a professional stand alone therapy, though there is an expectation that they will not do so until they have familiarized themselves with the work at this level and become used to the enhanced ability to channel Reiki energy given by the 2nd Degree attunements. Following my training with Gordon and Dorothy I was asked not to practice professionally for three months following the class, and this seems to me to be an eminently sensible approach, and one that I employ with my students. It takes about this long to really 'get on board' with the new abilities and practice and to allow this new level to really sink in and become an inherent part of your day-to-day routine.

## 3rd Degree

The 3rd Degree or Masters level can be taken after a period of time has passed from the 2nd Degree class, and is for those who really want to commit to Reiki, not just as a therapeutic discipline, but as a method to engage with as a way of life.

Training at this level is extensive, and cannot be completed simply over a weekend. It is my personal feeling that it is important that Masters within RJKD have a thorough grounding not only in the traditions of their own lineage, but a sound knowledge of the wider world of Reiki. This level of understanding was encouraged in me when I took my training and is something that I ask of my students now. Again, this requirement within the 3rd Degree training may not necessarily be common to all teachers of RJKD. I do feel that it can however help to really contextualize the students practice in relationship to the practice of others, and thus help them to define the particular stance of RJKD in terms of their own engagement with the system. Candidates for Reiki Masters training should also be familiar with working within the context of Reiki Therapeutics and submit approximately 20 case histories to their training Master. This enables their teacher to see that their understanding and commitment to this aspect of practice is grounded in a substantial body of experience and is ongoing. There is a lot of work to be done at this level.

Following the Masters attunement which raises the vibration of the seven major *chakras* and the giving of the fourth and final Reiki Symbol/mantra, students are introduced to a number of practices that again build on the work of the previous two levels, both of which are given time to be reviewed.

All four Reiki symbols are explored in some depth and the deeper meaning of the three 2nd Degree symbols is developed based in part on teachings derived from *Buddho-EnerSense*. In depth instructions are also given on how to use the fourth symbol/mantra to empower and enhance energy flow. It may well be as a consequence of the fact that the tradition of RJKD has up until recently been developed and carried by advanced spiritual practitioners all of whom are native Japanese speakers that the knowledge of the symbols held within the lineage is quite extensive.

There are a number of special breathing exercises introduced at this level. These are designed to not only increase the flow of energy through the subtle and physical bodies but also to maximize the student's sensitivity to energy both in the context of giving a treatment and also in enabling them to be very precise in their understanding of the activation of the body's energy matrix during the attunement processes. Again, mindfulness is developed with the student's attention being placed on the effects that the flow of energy has on various parts of the body, especially the hands. As a consequence of these exercises the sensations in the hands can be particularly intense and can in fact on occasion result in some physical pain or discomfort due to the flow of energy pushing the potential of the student to channel energy to greater heights.

Critical at this level of training is to establish a deeper understanding of the underlying philosophy of the lineage and how this impacts on and is a consequential development from continued meditation practice. *The Six Point Meditation*, introduced in its most simple form at 1st Degree, is extended further, building on the work done at both of the previous two levels. In the 3rd Degree students are expected to take their awareness during the meditation around various energy channels within the body following a specified sequence. As the mind and awareness moves, so does energy, and in this way it becomes possible to experience the accumulation of ki at any given point. This becomes an immensely useful tool for self-treatment, but moreover the practitioner finds that ultimately the movement of the mind and the energy develop a symbiotic relationship as they merge together.

*Vipassana* or *MindCheck* is also further developed, and in my classes considerable time is given over to exploring this practice with reference to various texts on the subject. This is an important practice as it is necessary for a Reiki Master to be particularly mindful of the arising of these mental states and the consequent emotions, especially negative ones. A Reiki Master must learn to 'walk their talk' and so needs to develop the ability to let go of negativity as quickly as possible.

Treatment practice is extended at the 3rd Degree. Self-treatment has further additional energy points to work on. This is linked to the ongoing application of *The Six Point Meditation* practice as the practitioner's awareness develops sensitivity to the energy and the energy moves with the movement of the mind. A similar approach is taken with the treatment of others. Principally based around the treatment style taught at 1st Degree, the practitioner now includes the application of Reiki to *chakra* points and other subtle energy points around the body in combination with an awareness of the movement of energy as it synchronizes with the breath.

The final part of the Reiki Master's training of course involves the learning of the attunement processes for all three levels. These are complex procedures and it is necessary to have an attitude of attention to detail in their application. The Reiki Master needs to develop sensitivity and awareness of energy flow to a high level for the performance of the attunement process as well as gaining an understanding of how the attunement process actually works. This is covered in detail. This ensures the correct and full transmission of energy to the student in the manner required for the continued connection to the lineage and line of teachers. All students, having learnt the attunement procedure, are expected, after a period of self-guided practice, to attune their own initiating Master at each level before being allowed to properly attune others.

✳

The newly created Reiki Master or teacher should be someone who has begun their own journey of compassion and wisdom for themselves and others. This needs to be expressed through their training, their practice and their experience of Reiki and developed in their everyday lives – this is the path of the Bodhisattva. In developing deeper insights into one's own mind, which ultimately leads to profound wisdom, the Reiki Master is led to a dedication to the helping of others enter the path to enlightenment. This is a great responsibility and should not be taken lightly. With the receiving of the Master symbol during the attunement process, the first step is taken in making a life-long commitment to one's students and to be available in times of need. It is the Reiki Master's personal responsibility to begin the process of development of compassion and wisdom through meditation from day one.

\*

It is appropriate to say something about *Buddho-EnerSense* at this stage and so the following is a brief outline of the four stages of training within this system. All students of *Buddho-EnerSense* are required to have received the Reiki Jin Kei Do attunements at the appropriate level to begin this training. Each level of training is taught in a graduated way to those already initiated into the system in accordance with its Tantric origins. This maintains a strong container and focus for the teachings. The system runs in tandem with the Reiki teachings, and can be accessed at various points, either following completion of training in Reiki or at a point where the *Buddho-EnerSense* system builds on the work done within the related level of the Reiki system. So a hypothetical student could chart their progress through the full teachings of RJKD in this way:

1st Degree – 2nd Degree – *Buddho-EnerSense* level 1 –
*Buddho-EnerSense* level 2 – 3rd Degree – *Buddho-EnerSense* level 3
– *Buddho-EnerSense* level 4.

The *Buddho* or *Buddho-EnerSense* system focuses on a meditation technique that amplifies the natural healing mechanisms of the body by utilizing the energy produced by the meditation process itself. The system also includes a set of exercises, called *Chi Nadi* that improve the physical health of the body and act as a catalyst for the practice of mindfulness. The *Buddho* meditation enables the practitioner to develop abilities in energy transfer to a higher degree and promotes a much more profound awareness of the subtle energy system. The *Chi Nadi* exercises involve slow relaxed movements that are reminiscent of *Tai Chi* and involves the dynamic tensioning of muscles to direct *chi* to various parts of the body. The training programme also includes breathing exercises that help to strengthen the lungs. The whole system promotes an increased level of vitality and all round health.

## Buddho-EnerSense Level 1

The *Buddho* meditation is introduced and the student receives an empowerment that activates four of the major *chakras*. The consequent increase in the student's awareness of the subtle vibrations of these energy centers becomes the focus of meditation at this stage. Two Sanskrit and three Tibetan symbols are taught for use in the three cycles of meditation at this level to enhance the flow of energy in the activated *chakras*. Instructions are given on two breathing methods for strengthening the lungs and *nadis* of the upper body. The first steps of the *Chi Nadi* exercises are also introduced.

## Buddho-EnerSense Level 2

Two further cycles are added to the three cycles of meditation from level 1 with further activation of the *chakras*. The next set of movements within the *Chi Nadi* exercise are demonstrated and two mantras (sounds) and yantras (geometric visual devices) used in healing and meditation are introduced. Distant healing techniques are taught and the origins of the 2nd Degree Reiki symbols are explored. An introduction to *nadi* or *marma* points is given along with methods of healing using these points by tuning into point pulse. The deepening of energy awareness and specific breathing exercises to achieve this are given.

## Buddho-EnerSense Level 3

This is the level required to be able to teach the previous two levels. Two further cycles are added to the meditation along with an empowerment to increase the activation of the *chakras*. More powerful mantras and yantras are introduced to deepen the state of meditation. Training is also given on the achieving of absorptive states (*dhyanas*) through a form of *Samatha* meditation derived from Theravadan Buddhism, and the factors observed in each of the absorptions. Further breathing exercises are given to increase awareness of subtle energy flow. The origins of the Reiki Master symbol are given at this level. The student is then taught the activation techniques for levels 1 and 2.

## Buddho-EnerSense Level 4

This stage involves advanced meditation techniques for deepening awareness to energy and the achieving of absorptive states. A further empowerment is given, and further breathing techniques are taught. Work with yantras is developed and a 4th level symbol for meditation and healing given. The use of *marma* points and *nadis* is expanded upon along with the initiation into higher meditation and object (sign). Students are taught how to achieve and stabilise the learning sign and introduced to the 12 links of the mind and the five constituents of being. The activation techniques for level 3 are learnt. The end stage of training in which the student can themselves teach level 4 is at the time of writing only available from the lineage head Dr Ranga Premaratna and two RJKD Masters teaching in Russia.

# 7

# The Guiding
# Principles of RJKD

The thought manifests as the word. The word manifests as the deed. The deed develops into habit. And the habit hardens into character. So watch the thought and its ways with care. And let it spring from love, born out of concern for all beings.

*The Buddha*

In all great spiritual and religious traditions there exists a set of admonitions or principles that sit at the center of the practice and act as a fulcrum for the particular tradition's teachings. There are the Five Pillars of Islam, the Ten Commandments, the Four Noble Truths and of course the Five Reiki Principles or Precepts. It is through aiming to achieve the state of human perfection that these types of ideals reveal to us, which ultimately leads us to engage in the practices of the tradition that are designed to enable us to surpass our state of mundane imperfection and thus realize our potential. This is to discover our true nature as spiritual beings and as an emanation of all-that-is. This is the primary aim of the Reiki Principles. These types of principles encapsulate the essence of the teachings in a powerful and direct way. When it comes down to it, with pretty much all spiritual traditions you could throw away everything except these fundamental points of philosophy, and still have a perfect and immutable path to perfection, and this is as much a truism for the Reiki Principles as it is of any other. It can be said that everything else within the tradition is just the vehicle that will transport you along the path. However, the vehicle – the teachings and practices – are necessary. To try to achieve the state of perfection required by the central principles without these is a task that is probably almost impossible for most of us. We all need a method. Through working with the Reiki Principles and using them as our guiding light, we cannot help but bring to consciousness our own profound wisdom mind, and in doing so we thus release our deeply innate compassion for all beings.

Regardless of lineage, the Reiki Principles are the common inheritance of every tradition within the Reiki family, and all stem from the same Principles that Mikao Usui first established to guide his students in the early part of the 20th century. These Principles, in whatever form they are given, have remained a much cherished and deeply respected aspect of the Reiki system – as is their due. As with the ideals of all spiritual traditions, the Reiki Principles embody eternal and immutable truths. They are not prone to change and they carry within them their own intrinsic self-worth and value. As Stephen Covey commented:

> Principles are deep, fundamental truths, classic truths, generic common denominators. They are tightly interwoven threads running with exactness, consistency, beauty, and strength through the fabric of life.

There have been a number of theories over the last few years as to the origins of the Reiki Principles or *Gokai* as they are known in Japanese, and as yet there is really no conclusive proof as to how Usui arrived at them. Perhaps we shall never know for certain. In the book *Reiki Fire* Frank Arjava Petter claimed that the Principles were derived from the Meiji Emperors *Imperial Rescript on Education.* Although this Rescript was held with the greatest of reverence in Japan right up until the end of World War 2, it is unlikely that this was the source of the Reiki Principles although there are similarities between the two. It is possible that Usui, in creating his own Principles, was influenced by Bizan Suzuki whose 1914 book *Kenzon no Gebri* contained a similarly worded set of precepts. Perhaps Usui was inspired by Suzuki. Perhaps it was the other way around. It is also possible that these Principles, as some have claimed, were derived from 9th-century Buddhist precepts. Whatever the origins, it would appear that Usui first started to use them in about 1915, though according to Hiroshi Doi, author of *Modern Reiki Method of Healing*, they only became a formal part of the system in 1922. A copy, in Usui's own hand, written in 1921 is believed to be still hanging in the shrine erected to him. It appears that it was Usui's practice to give the Principles to a student as their first teaching. Students would be asked to write the Principles out for themselves to help them focus their minds and so internalize their meaning. They would also be required to meditate on them regularly to reinforce this process.

There are many translations of the original Japanese Reiki Principles, and many versions of them have been extrapolated from these over the years since Reiki first appeared in the West. Probably the best known and also possibly the most beautiful in their simplicity and directness are those given to us by Hawayo Takata:

> Just for today, do not anger.
> Just for today, do not worry.
> Honor your parents, teachers and elders.
> Earn your living honestly.
> Show gratitude to everything.

This version of the Principles, whilst being derived from the Takata lineage, is sometimes also taught to students within RJKD.

They offer a clear, concise and easily remembered spiritual and worldly focus for the Reiki system. There is however a different version of the Principles, originally taught by Seiji Takamori that is given within RJKD, which I personally believe has, in some ways, a stronger resonance with not only the deeper meaning of Usui's original Principles, but also contains a method, if you will, to realize them in one's own life. There are two versions of the Principles within RJKD. Whilst the exact words may not be Seiji's, their intent and philosophic orientation certainly is. Ranga wrote the Principles based on his own understanding of Reiki and meditation but also after discussion with Seiji on their deeper meaning. Each say fundamentally the same thing, but with a slightly different flavor. Many teachers refer to both versions of the Principles, but I give them below in their final form:

> Be mindful each moment of the day;
> To observe the arising of greed, anger and delusion, looking
> deeper for their true cause.
> To appreciate the gift of life and be compassionate to all beings.
> To find the right livelihood and be honest in your work.
> To see within, the ever changing nature of your mind and
> body.
> To merge with the universal nature of the mind as Reiki flows
> within you.
> By following these ideals daily, your mind and body will
> transform and healing will follow.

The Reiki Principles are the standard by which we should live to bring balance to our work with Reiki in terms of our own spiritual growth and in the healing of others. By improving ourselves through living the Principles we can bring healing to our spiritual selves and so the Reiki energies can manifest lasting results within us. The deeper interpretation of the Principles in RJKD helps us to integrate Reiki and meditation within our lives. All of the Principles emphasize the quality of mindfulness by asking us to identify and acknowledge our own negative emotions as they arise by being acutely aware of our own thought process. As Ranga Premaratna has noted in regard to the Principles:

> All negative mental states can be encompassed in the three roots; greed, anger and delusion. Once these roots can be identified, we must look deeper to see what is the true cause of such mental states. The deeper cause behind the three roots is ignorance of the true nature of the self and the universe. By isolating ourselves into individual entities with 'self-consciousness', we do not see the universal nature of our existence and (thus) develop deep attachment to this unreal 'self' and the material things we accumulate. By being mindful every moment we can prevent such negative states from arising.

**The 1st Principle:** *Be mindful each moment of the day to observe the arising of greed, anger and delusion, looking deeper for their true cause.* Whether as a fleeting annoyance or as fully fledged rage we all know what anger is, we've all felt it. As each new day comes, and as each moment of each day comes, we need to bring a sense of mindfulness to the arising of such negative mental states such as anger. Anger is associated with greed and delusion, and all three are fundamentally interrelated. When we have desire (greed or attachment) and thus a need to control and this is unfulfilled, we develop anger and a state of delusion. Our minds become clouded and we cannot perceive things clearly and so we experience the state of delusion as reality. Anger then becomes our weapon of choice to force the other person, the world, the situation to give us what we want. It is an attempt to gain control, to be right, to have the last say and to be vindicated in our state of delusion and thus feed our greed. Anger stems from a strong desire to have things our own way. We want the world to work according to our agenda. We pontificate endlessly on the way that things should be, based on our own limited and entirely subjective view of the world. We want people to respond in a way that validates our sense of being right – a contrary view we believe is just wrong, and so we try to reform them and force them to see the error of their thinking.

As we work with Reiki and develop our abilities in mindfulness we begin to realize that negative mental states such as anger, frustration and irritation do not solve the problem. As this realization grows we become more inclined to apply wisdom and so take action in a positive direction to find a resolution. Our growing mindfulness allows us to catch the negative emotional states before they can take us on a path of self-destruction. As we begin to recognize the true nature of our minds and all phenomena, we also realize that negative, controlling mental states arise out of ignorance (or delusion) – the ignorance of the true nature of reality, and it is this ignorance that is the cause of our suffering. As Reiki sensitizes us to energy we start to notice the profoundly damaging effects that the arising of negative emotions has within us, both in terms of our state of mind and on the wellbeing of our physical bodies. The Buddha once noted that having anger towards someone is a bit like picking up hot coals to throw at your enemy – who gets burnt first? The antidote for the expression of anger is Reiki; the expression of compassion. We apply compassion (Reiki) to ourselves first of all to return us to a state of mental equilibrium, and then we feel compassion for whomever or whatever the object of our anger was, and realize that the anger or other negative emotion was self-generated. It did not come from outside of us, and was not given to us by anyone. We realize that we chose this path of anger for ourselves in the same way that we can also choose a path of compassion and forgiveness. Our mindfulness allows us to see the real root of all negative emotions – our own affronted egos. So we let go of our greed (attachment), which releases the need to be right and get what we want that can result in anger, and this dissolves delusion. In the beginning however, as anger arises, we need to find a safe mechanism for its release. Holding back such a powerful emotion, once it has arisen is immensely damaging. Indeed the arising of such an emotion expressed or not, is immensely damaging. Physiological and biological changes take place within the body. The heart rate goes up as does blood pressure along with an increase in energy hormones, adrenaline and noradrenaline. It can ultimately lead to pathological expressions of anger such as passive-aggressive behavior (getting back at someone without them knowing why) or a personality that feels the need to be constantly cynical, putting others down and criticizing everything. Skin disorders are a common manifestation of a perpetually angry state. So we need to find a way to work it out of our system so that it will not lead to a spiral of further anger and confrontation. By releasing the anger at the object of the anger, the other person, we simply create the circumstances for further anger to arise. My method is to simply walk away from the situation and take time out on my own or go for a walk, even for just a few minutes. Some find that writing their anger out and then destroying it works for them. The important thing is to find a method that works for you. Absolutely the worst thing you can do once this negative emotion has arisen is to not express it or endeavor to gain insight into why it arose or was triggered in the first place. It will just incinerate you from the inside out.

Worry and restlessness are two commonly felt mental states that can also arise due to our attachments, the arising of anger and our state of delusion. Sometimes having a cerebral cortex is not much fun. Imagination can litter our internal environment with every manner of fearful possibility. Worry and restlessness are the products of are habitual condition of either living in the past or the future. Moment by moment, most of us go through life being totally oblivious to what is happening to us and around us in the here and now. We live life in automaton mode. Our minds are constantly filled with memories of past events and projections into the future. Both have the same quality of being utterly unreal. Both are constructions of the mind that have no bearing on reality whatsoever outside of that which we choose to manifest from them based on our past conditioning. Our constant companions through life become worry and restlessness. We reach into the past, and project a worry that we have created from this memory into the future, bypassing the here and now which is where we have the choice over what will eventually become the new here and now. The uncertainties of the future, if we allow them, can run amok and develop into paranoia. We can end up so deeply entrenched in worry than we cannot see the possibility of a positive outcome. We can even become extremely angry over an imaginary will-o-the-wisp that we have created in an effort to hide our fear and so end up living in a profoundly unreal world as the state of delusion becomes magnified numbers of times over. All of this is a product of our attachment to the past and to the state of delusion. As we loosen the bindings of attachment and "hold everything with an open palm rather than a closed fist" we begin to reduce the suffering in our lives that is a consequence of our former strong attachment to things, ideas and people. This freedom from unnecessary suffering, from opening the closed fist of attachment, comes about through living in the here and now, by being mindful of causes and effects and through distancing ourselves from a reaction to the negative mental states when they arise. There is no point in regretting the past, or worrying about the future. Worry is ultimately a product of fear and based on a lack of faith or trust that the universe will provide for us exactly what we need at any given moment for our growth and development. As Shantideva pointed out

> If you can solve your problem, then what is the need of worrying? If you cannot solve it, then what is the use of worrying?

Regretting or worrying about the past gets us nowhere – it changes nothing. Worrying about the future is futile as what you fear may not actually come to pass. Indeed, it may well be that through your connection to the Universal Energy Field and the immensity of its/your creative abundance that your worries may indeed be the critical factor in manifesting that which you are worried about! As the negative energy of these negative mind states lowers our own vibration, it also impacts on the vibration of that which is around us, including our lives and so the negative mind state draws in negative situations. Mind is a magnet and we create our own reality by that which we think. This was illustrated beautifully when I gained an insight into the thinking of one particular lady. She said "I always feel bad even when I feel good, because when I feel good I know it will not be long until I feel bad again." As amusing as the quote is what a terrible way to go through life, but many people do this.

Worry and its related form in stress have a powerful effect on our immune systems. The more that we worry, the more damage we do to our own body as our natural defense mechanism begins to break down. Worry triggers many damaging chemical and physical changes in the body. Every single system in the body is affected by worry. The increase in adrenalin increases the flow of blood and oxygen to the brain and skeletal muscles. Blood clots faster, ready to repair the damage done in the 'fight or flight' state that the body is in. The liver begins to produce more cholesterol, which in turn raises your chance of a heart attack or stroke. Worry affects the skin and respiratory system. The list of negative physical consequences that can accrue from allowing worry into your life is astonishing!

A critical factor in the realization of the first Reiki Principle in our lives is the need to discover and acknowledge our own conditioning as separate entities from the Universal Mind or Consciousness. It is this ignorance of the true nature of the self that is the root of our desires and attachments and thus this Principle relates directly to the Buddha's Four Noble Truths. Through the practice of meditation, which concentrates and sharpens the mind we develop our mindfulness and so we can see the arising of anger and worry in every moment and the true cause of these mental states – and we can endeavor to let go. As we are mindful of the thought process we develop insight and understanding into the true nature of all phenomena, including other beings, and realize our oneness with everything. This allows us to choose to act and decide correctly, and thus compassion arises.

**The 2nd Principle:** *Be mindful each moment of the day to appreciate the gift of life and be compassionate to all beings.* It can sometimes be hard to appreciate the circumstances of one's life or indeed the gift of life itself when life is not going in the direction that we would like. Situations that we may find ourselves in can drag us down and we can become resentful or bitter about the way that our life is going, but there is a divine plan to it all. We of course have choice within this plan, and sometimes our choices can take us down experiential paths that in hindsight may lead us to regret our decision. The solution is not to become depressed about our circumstances but to refocus our approach to viewing the situation. No matter how long the tunnel it will eventually emerge into daylight and the night will always yield to dawn. Once we begin to realize that all is one and that nothing lasts forever, the true nature of the situation becomes more apparent. We can start to see our life as a series of opportunities and that even a wrong turn in the road will eventually lead us to further opportunities if we can be far-sighted enough to see past the mire that we may believe ourselves to be in at any given moment. This is not to suggest that we must be for ever holding out a hope and positive faith that 'things will get better when I can get out of the mess that I am in now' because this is to deny the true nature of the 'now' that we are in. The perceived 'mess' that we are in is in fact a wonderful, but transitory opportunity for further growth and the creative expression of our true nature. Once we can realize that every moment of our lives is a beautiful expression of the gift of life filled with abundance and opportunity we can begin to move forward with appreciation for our lives, moment by moment and with the real expectation that only further positive experiences and circumstances await us in the future. As Wallace

D Wattles noted in his book *The Science of Getting Rich*, "Gratitude brings your whole mind into closer harmony with the creative energies of the universe." This is so because we are an intrinsic part of the creative energy of the universe and to show less than gratitude for our lives, which is a manifestation of the universe, is to show less than gratitude towards ourselves.

As we apply Reiki and mindfulness in our lives we can drop the need for anger and worry through the realization of the destructive effects that these emotions have on our own bodies. Meditation combined with Reiki develops our sensitivity and eventually enables us to feel the effects of each thought that we hold. When we live in gratitude there is an accompanying sensation of expansion and energetic growth. When we feel sad, depressed or angry there is a feeling of constriction as if the world is 'closing in' on us. We can choose which way we want to feel. We need to choose to be grateful for all aspects of our existence. Harold Kushner in *The Healing Power of the 23rd Psalm* made this comment:

> Crabby people will find reasons to be crabby about the weather, whatever the day is like. It will be too hot or too cold, too rainy to go outdoors, or too dry to replenish the reservoir, and if one day is perfect, it will only get worse tomorrow. They complain not because of what the day is like but because of what they are like. By contrast, grateful people are grateful for the weather whatever it may be, remembering that April showers bring May flowers.

By developing our minds in meditation we can increase the space between each thought and thus realize our potential as human beings with the ability to become aware of our commonality with Universal Consciousness and so achieve enlightenment. Because of this capacity for developing our consciousness it is important that we take good care of our physical bodies, as it is our body that is the vehicle for our consciousness. As we develop appreciation for our physical existence and the life that we lead there arises a growing acknowledgement of the need for the expression of loving kindness. Firstly this is expressed for ourselves, and then through our connection to others we gain the desire to express this same feeling towards them also. This is true Reiki – the expression of unconditional loving kindness or compassion towards all beings.

This Reiki Principle delivers us to the heart of the Reiki system and the philosophy of RJKD. By releasing our negative emotions and bringing the quality of gratitude and appreciation for our lives into our day-to-day existence we can begin to recognize the suffering of others. With the dawning of this realization we can use our abilities with Reiki, enhanced by our practice of meditation, to feel and release the energy of compassion to ease this state of suffering. Mindfulness meditation or *Vipassana* helps us to remove our ignorance of the true cause of our own negative mind states. It tells us when we become angry and allows us the chance to release this feeling. We can thus see and feel our own suffering as well as the suffering that other people are experiencing. Practicing Reiki develops compassion as it opens our heart and teaches us to transform our negative emotions into positive life-enhancing ones. This gives us the opportunity to use our Reiki abilities to help heal ourselves and others.

Within the Takata lineage of Reiki we are asked to honor our parents, teachers and elders. In fact we need to honor everyone. On our journey through life we will come into contact with many people. The lives of some will converge with our own only fleetingly, whilst others may be in our lives for the duration. Regardless of this, everyone that we come into contact with is there to help us on our spiritual journey and to enable us to grow. For this reason alone it is important that we are not only grateful for the lessons that they have to teach us, but that we honor and respect their role within the divine plan for us all. If we reject these people and refuse to learn what it is that they have to offer then we limit our own potential to grow as spiritual beings. We are all faced from time to time with situations and people who, for whatever reason, we don't like or make us feel uncomfortable, or give rise to the emotions of anger or irritation or hatred. As it has often been said, these people are in fact our special friends as they provide us with such a crystal clear and beautiful opportunity for enormous growth. If we can learn, through our practice of Reiki and meditation, to overcome our negative inclinations towards these people, and generate within us the feeling of gratitude for their presence in our lives because of what we may learn from them, then we have made a giant step forward in our search for happiness and peace of mind. We may need to consciously forgive them for the wrongs that we feel that they have done to us, and this itself can be a hard journey to take. If we can take this first step however we can then take the next step of forgiving ourselves. If we can do this then we can feel the positive effects of such a process on our mental makeup, and we can generate the feeling of gratitude for the lesson learnt. As we become grateful for these people we are then able to feel their suffering, which is a reflection of our own, and again we have the opportunity for the arising of compassion for them. When life throws up these sorts of lessons we must never throw them away. They are priceless jewels that we should treasure and honor with great appreciation.

**The 3rd Principle:** *Be mindful each moment of the day to find the right livelihood and be honest in your work.* Right livelihood is that which allows us a true and full expression of our own innate creative abilities and enhances the physical and spiritual aspects of our lives. When we take employment, or engage in an activity on which we base our livelihood, we need to ask ourselves whether or not we are being honest with ourselves. Is this a real expression of what I am capable of? Is this a life-enhancing path for me? How much does it add to my growth as a human and spiritual being? We need to consider these issues carefully, and live according to our own inner promptings. Honest work has dignity and spiritual value. When we live a life of honesty, we tend to project honesty out into the world around us and thus others will respond accordingly. Our work should be conducive to spiritual practice and indeed should be an expression of that spiritual practice. We need to bring our mindfulness fully to bear on the tasks that we engage in. Whatever our livelihood entails, it is necessary for us to be consciously aware of the moment and engage fully in the task at hand. When we do this, we use the opportunity of working through the task as a chance to develop ourselves further, to become fully conscious in the present so that there is nothing to impinge on our minds other than the process of being in the here and now. Our work is an opportunity to engage in spiritual practice. As we pay attention to our work, we build our character and water the seeds of wisdom and compassion within us. When we engage in work that may be harmful to others, then it is a type of activity that cannot be considered as right livelihood. Dishonesty in the way that we pursue our livelihood is not conducive to mental peace and is therefore not conducive to spiritual practice.

It has been said that work is a somewhat like a Zen *koan*. A *koan* is an imponderable and impenetrable question that a Zen master asks his student. There is no rational or logical answer. The answer arises as one ponders the question and allows it to transform one's view of the world. So when we are employed, we need to set aside our status as an employee and realize that our real work is our spiritual practice. Whoever we work for, in our spiritual life we are self-employed. No one needs to know about this inner job – it is something we engage in 'on the side' and earn far more from it than a weekly pay-check.

Kumarappa had this to say:

> If the nature of the work is properly appreciated and applied, it will stand in the same relation to the higher faculties as food is to the physical body. It nourishes and enlivens the higher man and urges him to produce the best he is capable of. It directs

his free will along the proper course and disciplines the animal in him into progressive channels. It furnishes an excellent background for man to display his scale of values and develop his personality.

During a short period in my own life when I needed to find a job quickly I was confronted with the prospect of taking on grinding, repetitious work or earning good sums of money in the local slaughterhouse that is a big employer just outside of my home town. As a committed vegetarian of almost 20 years, the latter option, in spite of the lure of the huge wages, was simply not an option. Nor for me was the prospect of taking on work that would undermine my own sensibilities and desires to fulfill my creative instincts very appealing either. As I realized and fully appreciated the wonderful opportunity that had been presented to me, I set out to find work that would meet not only my financial needs, but allow me to express all that I am in a positive and life-enhancing way. With this attitude of gratitude firmly lodged within me, I literally stumbled across a job, in fact whilst taking a coffee break from job-hunting in a local vegetarian restaurant. The work that was offered met all of my requirements at that time. A job as a chef in the restaurant was handed to me on a plate over coffee. By accepting and appreciating the situation that I found myself in, in under an hour the universe had given me the livelihood that was most suitable to my growth and development at that time.

By maintaining an attitude of gratitude and being honest in our day-to-day lives, we increase our vibration to an incredible degree, and thus bring our minds into closer harmony with the energy of compassion that is our birthright.

**The 4th Principle:** *Be mindful each moment of the day to see within, the ever changing nature of your mind and body.* As we connect to and experience the universal nature of the mind through the development of mental clarity we can notice the energetic nature of our thought process as we observe the ceaseless flux of the arising and dissipating of our transitory thoughts. Through deep observation we become aware of the nature of our minds and bodies as a constant interplay of energy of different vibrations. As we continue our work with Reiki and meditation further clarity comes and we gain a profound understanding of the impermanence of all things and the inevitable dissolution of the physical body and the mental process.

By bringing the Reiki Principles into our lives as an active component of our spiritual makeup we are encouraged to daily transform our minds and bodies through the power of Reiki and our connection with the Universal Energy Field. Mindfulness develops and as we see the pointlessness of reacting in never-ending circles to our thought process we are able to stand back from ourselves and see the ever-changing energetic nature of our thoughts with clarity, the effects these thoughts have on our bodies and the rapid interplay of all physical phenomena. Our expanded awareness and understanding annihilates our ignorance of the Truth and thus our defilements. As we are transformed we let go of such negative mental states such as greed, anger, delusion, worry and restlessness (which are themselves defilements). We can then let go of all of our attachments, feel the expansion within our hearts and allow universal compassion to permeate all aspects of our existence.

**The 5th Principle:** *Be mindful each moment of the day to merge with the universal nature of the mind as Reiki flows within you.* As the energy of Reiki flows within us our vibration is lifted to a higher level, bringing us to a state of harmony with the Universal Energy Field. As we achieve this state of harmony the mental clarity that we develop through deeper and deeper observation of our lives, our bodies and our thoughts leads us inexorably to a state of identification with the energetic and impermanent nature of everything. As we develop ourselves further, a process that is enhanced by the continual flow of Reiki, we are able to experience in a direct and profound way the ultimate dissolution of our physical bodies and our mental processes. This is our ultimate aim and is known in Buddhism as the attainment of *nibbana* – the highest stage of mental purity. When we have achieved or attained the state of *nibbana*, the three primary psychological causes of all of our suffering; greed, hatred and delusion, and the effects of these causes are permanently and irrevocably uprooted. Suffering ceases. Thus we become aware of and recognize the only state of permanence that exists, the true nature of our being as the Universal Energy Field or God. The chunk of ice melts and once again becomes one with the vast ocean of Universal Consciousness. When we achieve this state, the cycle of *karma* and thus re-birth ceases.

\*

*By following these ideals daily, your mind and body will transform and healing will follow.* In working with the Reiki Principles I try to encourage my own students to bring them to mind at least once a day and in contemplating their meaning try to discover how this impacts on their own lives. The living and full expression of these Principles, which is supported by their practice of *Vipassana* meditation (described in the next chapter) is critical to the realization of the lineage philosophy; the development of wisdom and thus compassion and the integration of these qualities into our daily lives.

A final thought on the Reiki Principles of RJKD from Ranga:

> As we see the ideals are in a way sequential in the beginning of the practice. First we have to become aware of the negative mental states and see the root cause behind them. Then through the understanding of the mental process and the practice of meditation our minds become purer. With that purity of mind we begin to feel more compassionate towards ourselves and others.
>
> When this quality becomes well established, we seek to find work that does not hinder the spiritual path. When first we

can find such work and we do the work with integrity, peace of mind is attained. When life becomes peaceful we can establish and strengthen our healing and meditation practices. With the development of this strength, we begin to see our true nature. At this stage all of the ideals become co-existent, like the strands of fibre that make up a rope. The strength of the rope is in the proper entwining of the fibres.

# 8

# Meditation and the Development of Awareness

Irrigators guide the water; fletchers straighten arrows; carpenters bend wood; wise men shape themselves.

*The Dhammapada*

Meditation is a fundamental aspect of the teachings within RJKD and students are asked to engage with this practice throughout their training at all levels and to take it into their lives. It is within the practice of meditation that the serious work of developing the wisdom mind is done; to be combined with the heartfelt compassion of the Reiki flow. Symbiosis occurs when these elements are drawn together. My own experience of teaching Reiki is that sadly it is the practice of meditation that is the first to be dropped and then abandoned entirely by a significant number of students. Meditation is, at least in the beginning, hard work! It takes a high level of commitment, focus, desire and determination to continue with a practice that at first seems to be getting you nowhere and can impinge significantly on other aspects of your life. But to get the most from the system and to realize your own potential not only as a channel for Reiki but as a spiritual being on a spiritual journey back to consciousness of the true nature of the self, then meditation is a very important part of the practice.

So why meditate? What is really to be gained from it? According to Sogyal Rinpoche, author of *The Tibetan Book of Living and Dying:*

> The purpose of meditation is to awaken in us the sky-like nature of mind, and to introduce us to that which we really are, our unchanging pure awareness, which underlies the whole of life and death. In the stillness and silence of meditation, we glimpse and return to that deep inner nature that we have so long ago lost sight of amid the busyness and distraction of our minds.

Meditation can be regarded as a journey of discovery into the inner recesses of ourselves. It is a progressing in consciousness. As the psalmist writes, "Be still and know that I am God." In this stillness we can start to realize the infinity of our eternal being as an emanation of Divine Essence. We can touch and recognize our inherent nature and sublime state of oneness with the Reiki energy that we work with on the physical level. Whatever expectations we may bring to the practice, whatever our own goal may be, its ultimate purpose is to return us to the Source, where all that is, simply is, and with continued application this is where it will inevitably lead. When we take up the practice of meditation however, we do so generally with a particular objective in mind. Most of these objectives fall into one of the following main categories: health, stress prevention, self-realization and spiritual impulse. All of these are aims and desirable qualities that the meditations taught within RJKD aspire to realize. Regardless of the ultimate goal there are along the way many other benefits. The journey itself has much to offer in terms of our general state of mental and physical health. As already noted in the previous chapter, particular mental states, whether they are positive or negative, can have a significant effect on the physical body – there is a powerful bond between the mind and the body, and where the mind leads, the body will follow. When we engage in meditation and achieve a deep sense of relaxation, a sense of harmony and a profound feeling of being at peace, the body will respond in many beneficial ways. Lactate concentrations in the blood drop sharply and so reduce anxiety and stress levels. We can feel a sense of release and of acceptance as our worries dissolve and dissipate. There are numerous reports on the effectiveness of meditation in reducing hypertension, risk of heart disease, helping with addictive behavior and lowering blood pressure as well as increasing the ability to concentrate for longer periods of time, improving self esteem and creating a general sense of wellbeing and positivism in the meditator. The benefits of meditation in terms of our physical and mental health are numerous and significant. As Eric Harrison noted in his book *How Meditation Heals*, continued use of meditation as a healing therapy results in huge improvements in both a person's mental and physical health "…transforming people in ways that any psychologist or general medical practitioner would envy".

It is interesting to note that if we want to keep physically fit, we will engage in lots of exercise, lots of physical activity. We might go running or go to the gym, or swim or take up cycling. For keeping the mind in shape we should do exactly the opposite. When we start, our minds are moving much faster than our bodies – jumping, twisting, running, bending, etc and we need to stop it! When we can calm the mind and let it rest, then we are starting to develop our mind.

As we travel the road of meditation we must recognize that as wonderful and beneficial as the gifts we receive along the way are, there is a greater prize awaiting us. This prize is not something that we can ever grasp or know and say "I've made it!" and thus relinquish our commitment to the journey. The ultimate goal is something that is progressive and the stages of its realization are almost beyond human reckoning and description. As we begin a climb of the highest mountain we struggle and toil away, and then come to rest as we see what we believe to be the last peak just within our reach, only to realize that as we catch our breath, that as monumental a feat as we have accomplished, there is an even higher peak waiting. Yet rather than disappointment or resignation, the expansiveness that we have gained in achieving just this much propels us on to even greater heights.

Whatever our goals for taking up meditation, one of its most important aspects is to let go of our expectations. Let go of gaining the peak. We need to learn to just 'be' with the process, and enjoy it for what it is – a journey. In the beginning our minds wander and fill with all sorts of useless stuff that has nothing to do with the task at hand. We need to recognize that this is normal, it happens to everyone, and we should not berate ourselves for it. It is the natural process of the conditioned mind. If we start to get angry at ourselves for our initial failures in controlling our minds, then we are better off quitting the practice for that session rather than trying to pummel our minds into submission and force a state of iron-clad stillness upon it. This was my experience a long time before I came to Reiki. Instead of feeling at peace and a sense of serenity, I would simply get angry at myself for not making any progress and try to 'make' myself meditate. From what I have heard from numbers of students I don't think that mine was a unique experience. Instead of this, when the mind wanders it is important to simply catch it as soon as you can, acknowledge the thoughts that have arisen and gently and without judgment bring your focus back to the object of the meditation. For most people, progress with meditation is a slow and gradual process. In our 'I want it now!' societies we are conditioned to expect immediate results and we get immensely disappointed when this doesn't happen with meditation. It is at this point that most people give up and proclaim that they can't meditate and that it is impossible for them to stop their minds from wandering. Patience and resolve are the answers. It could be weeks or even months before a practitioner starts to feel that they are making any headway. It takes regular and sustained practice. It is also no good getting half way up the mountain, clapping yourself on the back for doing so well, and as a reward pitching your tent and giving yourself a few weeks off. Meditation is not like riding a bike either. Imagine what it would be like if, having learnt to ride a bike, you then don't get on one again for a few months or maybe years and then are forced to bike to work one day because the car won't start. You find that you have almost completely forgotten how to ride the bike at all! You can sort of remember how to do it, but you can't get balanced. This is what happens with meditation if you put it down for too long – you can recall the mechanics of how to do it, and the experiences that you had, but you pretty much have to start all over again.

The practice of meditation needs to become at least a daily if not moment-by-moment experience. Through committing to this practice, and so developing our minds, our consciousness, and connecting with more and more rarified states of energetic being, we can connect and resonate with the Reiki source and our abilities as channels for Reiki in a much deeper and more profound way. Eventually there is no 'doing' in meditation; meditation simply arises. Meditation is as much an energy discipline as is the channeling of Reiki through the hands. As we meditate and make progress, we raise our own vibration closer and closer to the vibrational frequencies of the Universal Energy Field. In this way we expand our abilities with Reiki. We begin to imprint within our own energetic profile a higher state of resonance and so the practice of meditation goes hand in hand with the practice of channeling Reiki as they are mutually supportive disciplines. Through committed use of Reiki and meditation we break the bonds that tie us into the physical world and keep us in a state of deluded suffering. We let go of our attachments and come home to our essential natures.

There are many ways or methods of meditation, possibly as many as the benefits that can be accrued from the practice. In line with the philosophy of the lineage and to reinforce the gains made through the other methods within the lineage canon, a number of skillful means within the practice of meditation are taught to students. These are not exclusive to any one particular level or degree in our system of Reiki, but are given in a simple form at the start of training and generally become progressively more complex as the student moves through to the 2nd and 3rd Degrees.

## *Metta Bhavana* or Loving-kindness

*Metta Bhavana* is the original name of this meditation practice and comes from the Pali language. *Metta* means (universal) love or friendliness or kindness. It is a heartfelt emotional outpouring. *Bhavana* means cultivation or development. So the practice is aimed at the cultivation of love and kindness that leaves us in an expanded and beautiful state of mind. It is the expansion of the self beyond all selfish concerns to take an active interest in the welfare of all other beings without exception.

The cultivation of loving kindness is one aspect of a larger practice that is known as *brahma vihara*, which means 'the godly or divine abode'. The other three practices are; the development of compassion (*karuna*), sympathetic joy (*mudita*) and equanimity (*upekka*).

There are a number of variations to this powerful self-and-other-healing practice of loving kindness, and many books on Buddhist meditation will include at least one method for you to try. It was first taught by the Buddha more than 2500 years ago and is recorded in the *Metta Sutta*. In its commonest form there are five stages. The method employed within RJKD, whilst sharing the objective, is approached slightly differently. Here is the five-stage method:

The first stage asks that we feel love and compassion for ourselves. We are the focus of the meditation. We begin by bringing our awareness to ourselves and generating feelings of peace and tranquility within us. Then we let these feelings grow and become feelings of strength and confidence and finally we feel love and compassion in our hearts. We can see this as a golden light flooding the body, or feel it simply as an expansiveness in the heart. We can use a phrase such as "I am now filled with love and serenity" that we can say internally to reinforce this feeling. The specific visualization or words are not as important as the feeling that is generated – whatever tools work, these we use.

In the second stage we can bring our attention to someone close to us – a friend or relative maybe. We start by bringing them to mind as vividly as we can and then pay attention to all of their good qualities: their generosity, or smile, or patience or enthusiasm – everything that we can think of. In doing this we make a connection with them and we notice the positive emotional state that arises in us as a consequence. Again this can be reinforced by the repetition of an appropriate phrase such as "May they be well, happy and healthy." We might also like to visualize our love for our friend flowing from our hearts as a beam of brilliant white or golden light and then either surrounding them or connecting with their heart.

For the third stage we think of someone that we are pretty much indifferent to. We don't like them, but we don't dislike them either; they are essentially neutral. It could be someone that we pass regularly in the street, or who lives a few doors down from us. So we bring this person to mind and we begin to reflect on their humanity. We acknowledge that they, like us, are searching for peace and happiness in their lives. In doing this we can share in their desire and so feel our connection with them. Along with internally repeating a suitable phrase this then allows us to generate a feeling of warmth towards them, which we then transform into love and compassion and feel it again as an expanding of the heart as we send out beams of love to this person.

The fourth stage is often the most difficult. Here we think of someone that we actively dislike – an enemy. It doesn't matter why we dislike them, but it is important that we do dislike them.

The more we dislike this person the better for our practice. In the beginning it is essential to try to catch our thoughts and not get carried away with plowing the fields of hatred. Everything sown will ultimately grow, so again we focus on their humanity and their need for love and compassion and understanding. We recognize that they too are searching for the answers, and feeling their way towards happiness out of the suffering that they are experiencing in their lives. As our sense of commonality with them grows, we can again begin to feel a heart connection to them. Even if we have to fake it initially, we can repeat a phrase that wishes them well, and visualize beams of love and light going out towards them from our heart. This will ultimately give way to a sense that our practice is real and that we are no longer faking it. We think of them positively and send out our *metta* to them as well.

In the final stage we can think of all four people together: our self, our friend or relative, the neutral person and the enemy and we extend feelings of love to all of them. Then we push these feelings out further to everyone around us, and then everyone out in our neighborhood, our town, our country and to everyone throughout the world. We hold the sense of waves of compassion and love spreading out from our hearts to all beings everywhere. Finally we relax out of the meditation and end our practice.

The practice of *Metta Bhavana* and the expression of *metta* or loving kindness is one that is highly esteemed within Buddhism. In fact the expression of love or loving kindness is a requirement of all spiritual and religious traditions, though it may be expressed in different ways and through different means. The development of this quality is central to the realization of the philosophy of RJKD within our lives. Its focus is on giving oneself selflessly to others and to developing the desire to have all beings – everyone – released from their state of suffering. As we progress we need to endeavor to bring this awareness, this selfless attitude, into our daily lives. It needs to be a part of our interaction with our families, with our colleagues at work, with those we meet casually, and with those we would rather keep away from. It needs to become an attitude of mind that permeates all aspects of our lives. The force of this requirement is expressed powerfully by the Buddha in the *Metta Sutta:*

> Even as a mother watches over her child, her only child, as long as she lives, so truly, for every being arouse a boundless heart. Arouse a heart of boundless kindness for all things and all creatures – upwards and downwards and across the world. Unhindered, free of hate and enmity.

As practitioners of Reiki, when we engage in this method and use the types of visualization described above, we begin to notice a powerful surge of energy into and through our heart *chakras*. When we visualize beams of light or pure gold going from our heart to that of another, we are empowering this visualization with Reiki, which begins to flow unhindered towards the object of our meditation. The effect of this meditation is enhanced significantly by our abilities as Reiki channels and can impact dramatically on the person whom we are focused on. In this way we start to bring to realization that which we are instructed to do in the 2nd and 5th Reiki Principles. We begin to appreciate ourselves and our lives and develop kindness to all beings. As this feeling grows we become empowered with the desire to pursue this work of helping others and expressing compassion for their state of suffering through the use of our Reiki hands and further in our practice of meditation. The expressing of love has been likened to the merging of a river with the ocean and in so doing losing its identity and becoming one with the ocean. My own experience of practicing *Metta Bhavana* is that as the energy of love and compassion (Reiki) first builds within me and then spreads outwards to others close to me and onwards to eventually encompass the whole of the physical universe, there is a critical dissolution of my own sense of being separate from the rest of the physical world. My physical being, firstly seems to melt and become transparent and ethereal and then the rest of the physical world seems to follow so that all that remains is a sense of being one with the whole universe as an ocean of pure love. This is the goal of our practice.

## Six-Point Meditation

*The Six-Point Meditation* is one that is fundamental to the tradition of Reiki as expressed within RJKD. It is essentially a simplified form of the *Buddho* meditation that Usui used during his retreat on Mt Kurama that lead to his self-generated attunement and empowerment to the stream of Universal Energy. When we engage in this meditation we are engaging with a method that takes us to the heart or core of the entire Reiki system. We meditate on the flow of Reiki energy itself. *The Six-Point Meditation* has three distinct phases or stages. The simplest, most stripped down method is taught at 1st Degree and it then becomes progressively more complex at the 2nd and 3rd Degrees as the mind, facilitated by the use of a Reiki symbol is directed to various energy centers and *nadis* within the body's energetic makeup. As we engage in this meditation we become progressively more aware and attuned to the nature of the flow of Reiki energy through our bodies. We develop our sensitivity to and awareness of the flow of energy and this is one of its objectives. We can become acutely aware of the effect that it has on various aspects of our energy body as well as upon our physical body. As we delve deeper and deeper into this experience we can gain profound insight into the nature of the Reiki energy itself as we sense and feel on a primordial level its deep and inherent compassionate nature. Engaging in this meditation is an opportunity to fling wide the doors to the infinite ocean of all that is and will ever be. As with the repeated practice of hands-on Reiki, the repeated use of *The Six Point Meditation* will also increase our abilities to channel Universal Energy. It is a purifying mechanism. When we do the meditation, Reiki energy flows in abundance and it is a typical experience to feel our hands tingling and heating up during the course of the meditation. As we practice further we can find that this sensation of energy and thus healing can be found anywhere on or in our bodies simply through placing our awareness at a specific site. Remember, energy follows thought. My own experience is that in engaging in this meditation my whole body becomes a Reiki dynamo! I get very hot and there is a sense of energy pouring from me in every direction from every part of my body at once.

*The Six-Point Meditation* can be approached in two ways. Firstly as a daily, sitting meditation practice, and secondly as a method for turning every Reiki treatment that we do, whether on ourselves or on someone else into a form of meditation with the hands.

What do we mean by meditation with the hands? In many spiritual traditions – Reiki being merely one of them – there is a profound teaching on the nature of suffering and the way to alleviate suffering in the world. Universally there is an admonition that we need first of all to work on ourselves, relieve our own suffering, become healthy and whole on a physical and spiritual level and realize our own need for compassion, forgiveness and love. This is one of the reasons that we engage in daily self-treatment with Reiki. When we first come across this concept it may appear to be selfish and of no use in easing the suffering of others. Of course as we progress on our spiritual journey, we realize that the purer and more in tune with our own spiritual nature that we are, the more we have to offer to others and the greater will be our contribution in easing the suffering and pain in the world. When we give a Reiki treatment to someone else it is clearly the purpose of the exercise for the recipient to take the opportunity to restore their own sense of health and wholeness. Yet, we as the Reiki channel use this opportunity to engage in our own meditation practice. Once the treatment is underway, and with a sense of mindfulness for the wellbeing of the recipient we do our *Six Point Meditation* in part for our own benefit. We use this opportunity whilst the energy is flowing to take another step on our own journey. The consequence of this for the recipient is that as we enter deeper and deeper states of meditation, we remove ourselves more and more from engaging on an intellectual and ego-driven level with the mechanics of the Reiki treatment going on under our hands. Our intuition becomes heightened and we are more easily able to respond to the various energy fluctuations within and around the body of the recipient. We bring ourselves to a state of unity with the eternal now, and disengage from any notions of what we believe might be wrong with the recipient, what caused the problem, what the recipient needs on a healing level and what we as an individual can do about it. Our egos become pushed out of the equation and so the Reiki energy flows in abundance to precisely where it is needed, unimpeded by our little self and its desire to help based on its limited understanding of the healing process. As we engage in our meditation for our own benefit, but with the realization that it is also aiding the recipient in numerous and profound ways, the more we remove ourselves from the process of giving a treatment and so the more the energy can flow and the better the experience for the recipient. Helping ourselves in this way first optimizes our ability to help others. For me, this is one of the most beautiful experiences of the entire Reiki system and goes deeply into the fundamental theoretical basis of many spiritual and religious traditions.

In meditating on the energy flow, either as a formal meditation practice or whilst giving a hands-on treatment, we are developing two important qualities that we need on our spiritual journey: concentration and insight. In Buddhist terms these are known as *Samatha* (one-pointed concentration) and *Vipassana* (insight or mindfulness). *Samatha* and *Vipassana* – concentration and insight – meditation are important elements of the journey for all serious students of RJKD. The two approaches are mutually supportive, but we do need to be aware of the differences between them.

## Concentration Meditation (*Samatha*)

In a *Samatha* meditation we take one thing or one object as our focus, the purpose of which is the stilling of the mind through letting go. It involves one-pointed concentration on the particular chosen object – in this case, with the practice of *The Six Point Meditation*, on the flow of energy. In engaging in this meditation as the mind becomes totally absorbed in the energy flow we develop calmness, tranquility and serenity through deeper levels of one-pointedness. When we are concentrating correctly, we simply rest our mind on the object (energy) and let go of everything else in the universe. When we talk of concentration, what we are not alluding to is the repression of the mind. This suggests that in trying to concentrate we are forcing the mind to be still and thus setting up a mental tug of war between the mind's desire to remain still and its tendency to wander. Such a tug of war is exhausting and defeats the objective of the practice. The nature of concentration is detachment. To achieve this we simply rest our mind on the energy flow and return it there every time it wanders off. Eventually, the mind's tendency to wander weakens and ultimately disappears altogether. More advanced practitioners of this type of meditation experience states known as 'absorptions' or *jhana's* in Pali. This is the state of being deeply absorbed in the object of the meditation. This can lead to a profound and indescribable sense of peace but the mystical states that can arise in this context, whilst highly pleasurable and deeply relaxing, need ultimately to be relinquished, as they are not the final goal. As we develop our sensitivity to energy flow and our abilities in one-pointed concentration, we also need an awareness that the ultimate goal of meditation is to achieve enlightenment or oneness with the Universal Energy Field or God. This cannot come from a Concentration/*Samatha* practice. For this we need *Vipassana*. There are however two important ways in which a *Samatha* practice can help us on this ultimate journey. Firstly, as we develop this sense of letting go – detachment – we are more easily able to renounce desire and aversion. Secondly, we develop our one-pointed concentration and mental ability to a high degree which is necessary for effective *Vipassana*/Insight practice. So within the context of our Insight meditation, we practice *Samatha* or one-pointedness.

## Insight/Mindfulness Meditation (*Vipassana*)

Insight meditation is designed to purify the mind through the complete eradication of mental impurities and so achieve a complete healing, not just of the body, but of all human suffering, whether it is mental, emotional or physical. In a general sense we can say that Insight/*Vipassana* meditation is a practice of awareness and clarification whilst Concentration/*Samatha* meditation is a practice of calming and the development of one-pointedness. Insight meditation is about seeing things as they really are. It is a reflective activity where we are encouraged to look at our own lives, noticing the movements of both body and mind and whether our minds contain wholesome or unwholesome thoughts. Through self-observation we achieve self-transformation. Within the practice of *The Six Point Meditation*, as we bring our one-pointed concentration to bear on the energy flow, we are also keeping our perception of reality rooted and fixed in the moment. The energy upon which we focus continually ebbs and flows, arises and passes away. Within each moment the energy changes and transforms different aspects of our being – everything is in a state of flux. In observing the energy and penetrating deeply into its nature we become aware not only of the continually changing characteristics of the energy – the state of impermanence, but also of the deep interconnection between the mind and the body.

The state of the body and all of its functions is contingent upon the movement of the mind and thus energy. Our awareness (mind) is focused on the movement of energy through the body and the effect that this has upon it, and we recognize that although the body and mind are interconnected, they are not identical. The mind is in charge and orders the body around in the same way that it influences the flow of Reiki. Energy will follow our thoughts just as our thought follows the energy. So we realize what a profound impact on firstly our bodies and then on our lives in general the mind has. We can become aware of our thought process, moment by moment and begin to see it for what it is — a stream of thoughts that are just that and nothing more. We watch the arising and passing away of our thoughts and note their qualities, and then let them go and focus once again on the movement of energy. In doing so we achieve a state of mental clarity which allows us to reflect on the way that our lives are pulled in different directions by this stream of thoughts that continually arise within us, and we start to realize that we spend much of our lives like this. Almost all of the time we live in an unreal world of memories of the past and projections into the future, and all of these memories and projections have the inherent quality of impermanence. We begin to develop an intense awareness of the state of impermanence of everything. Yet the thoughts can also be conditioned by the movement of the body and so we arrive at the common root of both and so life becomes characterized by increased awareness, self-control and peace as we begin to see the true nature of everything. Reality we discover is to be found only in the now — moment by moment. As we become more mindful of our minds and bodies in the here and now our lives become vastly different to the life that we might lead that is devoid of mindfulness. Continuity may give the illusion of permanence, but this just masks the reality of impermanence. The ego doesn't like impermanence and would rather believe in the illusion that is created by continuity. To acknowledge impermanence is to acknowledge the ultimate extinguishing of the ego itself.

Insight meditation is now being used by prison inmates as a method to increase self-esteem and self discipline and to reduce feelings of depression, hostility, helplessness and hopelessness in several large prisons in the US, India, New Zealand and the UK. As a consequence of the practice one prison in the US has reported a sharp decrease in drug and alcohol addiction, whilst another in India has claimed that a special isolation room that is usually reserved for the most troublesome prisoners is now nearly always empty. The benefits for the prisoners have proven to be so dramatic that in many places the prison staff have also taken up meditation.

✳

Within *The Six Point Meditation* then we have two distinct, but interwoven threads to the practice. We engage in this meditation, firstly to develop our abilities in and sensitivity to the flow of Reiki energy, but also to bring us to the realization of the true nature of all mental states and physical processes. To achieve this however the ability to sustain the mind in the state of one-pointed concentration is necessary. This seems simple enough in theory but there is an inherent dichotomy here. *Samatha* practice requires that the meditator brings the mind back to the focus of the meditation – energy flow, each time that it wanders. *Vipassana* practice however requires that the meditator take note of the activity of the mind and the movement of the energy and acknowledge whatever is to be found. To resolve this contradiction it becomes necessary to develop the powers of concentration to a degree that will result in the noting mind being more powerful, more attentive and faster than the wandering mind. In this way it can overwhelm the wandering or thinking mind and take note of its qualities very quickly and return to the object of the meditation. If the noting mind is not developed sufficiently, then the wandering mind takes control and concentration temporarily evaporates. As concentration on the energy flow deepens however, the mind develops the strength to note the qualities of the wandering mind and the arising and ceasing thought process very quickly and attentively. When the speed and attentiveness in noting the thoughts is highly developed, the stream of extraneous thought slows down and so concentration can become deeper and deeper.

The practice of one-pointedness as a singular meditation activity gives rise to profound experiences of serenity and peacefulness but these are in themselves entirely transitory. Once the meditation ceases, the state of peace can disappear as normal life begins to impinge upon the mind's calmness. The practice of Insight meditation needs ability in one-pointedness for it to be successful; otherwise the wandering mind will simply lead the way. The realizations that come from Insight meditation however are lasting and permanent. They do not evaporate in the way that the state of peace engendered through Concentration meditation does. So in developing both the twin strands of our meditation practice it is hoped that we can come to a point in which we realize the true nature of existence, let go of our attachments and thus the state of peace and serenity becomes our constant companion.

## MindCheck

*MindCheck* is a RJKD tool to evaluate the progress of our meditation that was developed by Ranga Premaratna and allows the practitioner to observe with clarity the arising of wholesome and unwholesome thoughts. It is in some senses an Insight/ *Vipassana* practice in its own right as it reinforces and links in with the 1st, 4th and 5th Reiki Principles where we are asked to pay attention to and discover the root of the arising of greed, anger and delusion and the impermanence of these and all other mental states, the recognition of which ultimately leads to the attainment of an enlightened state of being. If we are to fully explore these Principles in our lives then the practice of a method such as *MindCheck* is necessary. In the beginning we may not have the clarity to detect the arising of these thoughts but as we become more aware, we have the power to let them go as soon as they arise. As we explore the arising of negative mind states at first we believe that they arise as a consequence of external factors: he shouted at me and so I am angry – it is his fault. She has a bigger piece of cake than me so I am jealous – it is her fault. As we look deeply at the roots however we begin to take responsibility for the arising of these thoughts. When we feel sad, it is because we are responding on the basis of our conditioning to that which is triggering the sadness, but did not create the sadness. The sadness, anger, hate, jealousy are all generated from within. We create these feelings ourselves. As we realize that it is our own conditioned response mechanism that is creating the negative emotional state, then we give ourselves choice and control. This is not to say that it is easy to exact control. It is very difficult to start with and as Ranga has noted "we are powerless to stop the force of conditioning which drives the thought process in the unwanted and harmful direction". At the start, we may be aware of the fact that our anger is self-generated, and we can watch ourselves become angry, but the force of the conditioning still drives us on in the harmful direction – it takes determination and sustained practice to let go of such strong emotions. We need to learn to guard the sense doors. The six senses through which all of our mental states are triggered are hearing, smelling, tasting, feeling, seeing and thinking. As Ayya Khema pointed out in her classic *Who Is Myself? A Guide to Buddhist Meditation* when we see a piece of chocolate, the eye only sees a brown shape. It is the mind that thinks "Ah chocolate! That tastes delicious – I want a piece!" So the mind creates the condition for the arising of desires (attachments) that could ultimately lead to the feeling of satisfaction if we get the chocolate or jealousy or resentment if someone else eats the last piece before we do. Our senses give the mind material that it interprets in many ways based on its past experiences of those same or similar materials. Everything becomes categorized and is labeled with various emotional tags: nice, bad, horrible, delicious, funny, fearful, etc. In this way we create attachments. Attachment formation comes about through the repetition and development of sensory escape from suffering: we run away if we don't like it or we grasp it if it makes us feel good. As we live in and worry and get angry about the past and the future, we learn to distance ourselves from pain by indulging in practices that temporarily alleviate our pain or desires but do nothing for the long-term consequences of having attachments that recycle the state of suffering in our lives. We can drink too much or eat too much, watch television or make love, and having found that these mechanisms work, even if only in the short term, we repeat them over and over again every time we feel the need to escape from something. So we develop habits that become attachments and these become the basis of our sense of who we are as we identify with our habitual behaviors and preferences and so we stifle and distort our ability to see clearly. *MindCheck* gives us the opportunity to realize the nature of our attachments that stem from our emotions. It doesn't matter whether the emotion is positive or negative, what matters is that we become aware of it and what created it.

*MindCheck* for 1st Degree students is in a form that will allow a very gentle introduction to the practice and requires a reflective approach at specified times. By the 3rd Degree this practice should be taken on board as a continual process of reflection and self-evaluation to enable us to break down our attachments. We start to live in the here and now. This takes time and patience with ourselves, but with the continual use of *The Six Point Meditation* in our lives, our one-pointed concentration develops to a level where the reflective process required in *MindCheck*, either from a specific time from which we evaluate previous mental conditions, or in the moment as the mental condition arises, becomes easier and eventually second nature.

✳

As we progress in our meditation we develop not only the states of calmness and tranquility of mind but we also purify the mind of defilements and negative influences such as lust, hatred, jealousy, ignorance, restlessness, indolence, envy, worry and sensual desire. In their place we develop the qualities of compassion, confidence, wisdom, mindfulness, concentration and deeply penetrative insight. It takes work and sustained effort but the many benefits that will accrue are worth it in the end.

# 9

# Energy Cultivation

Be soft in your practice. Think of the method as a fine silvery stream, not a raging waterfall. Follow the stream, have faith in its course. It will go its own way, meandering here, trickling there. It will find the grooves, the cracks, the crevices. Just follow it. Never let it out of your sight. It will take you....

*Sheng-yen*

The energetic disciplines of *Qi Gong*, *Tai Chi* and Yoga, whilst distinctly separate practices from Reiki, do have something of a resonance within the larger teaching of *Buddho-EnerSense* as each have factors in common with the practice of *Chi Nadi* within this tradition. *Chi Nadi* exercises are not taught within the Reiki system, but it is appropriate to draw on the reasoning and philosophy of the *Chi Nadi* approach and to admit this into the Reiki system as a way of introducing a style of energy work that may serve to prepare those students who ultimately go on to train in *Buddho-EnerSense*. Of course, whether they go on to learn the *Buddho-EnerSense* method or not, the introduction of specific skillful methods into the Reiki canon is very beneficial for the practitioner in any case. At 1st Degree Ranga has introduced a *Qi Gong* method called *The Seven Purifying and Strengthening Breaths*. At 2nd Degree a very simple energy awareness/palm activation exercise is taught that utilizes one of the Reiki symbols, whilst at 3rd Degree there are four focused breathing methods that involve the tensing and relaxing of various parts of the body and specific muscle groups. All of these methods, whilst unrelated in some senses, do serve to strengthen, harmonize and increase energy flow within the body as well as to sharply focus energy at specific points and develop sensitivity within the student.

One of the main aims of energy cultivation exercises such as these is to teach the student how to feel energy, and as the energy harmonizes and comes into balance, to nourish and develop the body and mind. This becomes a critical factor at 3rd Degree when the prospective Reiki Master needs an acute sensitivity to energy for the successful completion of the RJKD attunements. The four exercises taught at this level are specifically focused on developing this quality. Of course a developed sense of energy flow and fluctuation is also important at 1st and 2nd Degree, particularly when the student intends to work with Reiki as a therapeutic tool on others. In taking up the energy cultivation practices at 1st Degree with *The Seven Purifying and Strengthening Breaths* the student is encouraged to develop the ability to store energy in the lower abdomen (*Tan Tien* in Chinese and *Hara* in Japanese), which is the body's energy center. At 2nd Degree students are expected to continue and deepen their practice of *The Seven Purifying and Strengthening Breaths*. This can possibly be aided by incorporating into the practice the use of the Reiki symbols to increase energy flow. The energy awareness/palm activation exercise taught at this level, which includes the use of the Reiki Power symbol, also brings a student's focus to the specific flow of Reiki through the body and ties in with their practice of *The Six Point Meditation*. With the four energy cultivation exercises taught at 3rd Degree, students learn to concentrate this vital energy – *ki*/Reiki – at particular spots or points in a very focused and precise way. This produces an extraordinarily powerful flow of energy that can then be utilized in the attunement process. This is done by 'forcing' energy in particular directions through the dynamic tensing and releasing of certain parts of the body. In the practice of *Tai Chi* or other martial arts, there are points within the form that require a sudden explosive release of *chi* in a particular direction via a particular part of the body – an open palm or a fist for instance. At these moments, coupled with correct breathing and focused intent, momentary tensing of the muscles takes place to drive the *chi/ki* in the required direction, in the same way that is necessary within the RJKD 3rd Degree exercises. Breath work is critical to all of these methods and it is worth having a look at how the use of the breath contributes to and strengthens the ability to channel and transmit energy.

Practices such as *The Seven Purifying and Strengthening Breaths* and the other methods within RJKD, help to instill deep natural breathing within the practitioner, whilst the breathing itself helps to develop personal *ki* and the ability to channel Reiki. One of the aims of this type of energy work is to train the practitioner to breathe correctly. This may sound like a perfunctory exercise, but for most adults it requires a great deal of concentration which of itself makes the process a form of meditation. The Chinese classic the *Tao Te Ching* notes:

> Can you keep the soul always concentrated from straying? Can you regulate the breath and become soft and pliant like an infant?

When we work at this over a period of time it is possible for adults to achieve this state so that the body does indeed become soft and pliant and the breath flows naturally and deeply from the pit of the stomach, or *Tan Tien/Hara*. At the start of our lives we breathe from the belly as if we are still centered on the umbilical chord. As we age, our breathing rises to our chests so that most adults believe that breathing is somehow controlled by the chest muscles. When we are able to sink our breathing back down to our abdominal area where it belongs, *chi*, *ki* or Reiki flows naturally and in abundance.

In a sense we could say that the breathing aspect of these exercises is a form of *pranayama*. *Prana* is the Indian word for *chi* or *ki*, whilst *ayama* means, amongst other things; extension, regulation, restraint and control. All of these qualities are utilized within the RJKD energy cultivation practices. This is most significantly the case with the 3rd Degree exercises, but in all of them there is developed an understanding of the connection between energy, the breath and the mind or consciousness, as they are all intrinsically interlinked. Energy, as we know, is focused where we place our attention or consciousness, but consciousness will also follow energy. In yogic teaching we learn that when the breath is still, energy is still and thus so is consciousness/mind. The reverse therefore must also be true. When we utilize our breath and move our consciousness then energy must follow. Through the breath we can stabilize or activate the movement of energy in a powerful way. Correct breathing is a dynamic process.

Our practice of meditation helps tremendously in this process as whatever happens in the mind influences the breath. When we are stressed or excited, our breath becomes shallow and quick. When we are relaxed and peaceful it is deeper and quieter. So to have mastery over the circulation of energy within us and to maximize our capacity as channels for Reiki we need to have mastery over our minds and our breathing. If we act negatively, we disturb the equilibrium of the mind. The consequence of this is that our breathing becomes shallow and not only does our personal energy exude from our bodies, but our ability to channel Reiki is also hindered. As we engage in correct and deep breathing through the daily energy cultivation exercises – which should then carry over into our everyday lives, we support our practice of meditation and help to bring our minds to a state of peace and harmony and so energy can flow in abundance. As the Reverend Thich Nhat Hanh has noted:

Breathing and knowing that we are breathing is a basic
practice. No one can be truly successful in the art of
meditating without going through the door of breathing.
To practice conscious breathing is to open the door to
stopping and looking deeply in order to enter the domain of
concentration and insight...Conscious breathing is the way into
any sort of meditative concentration.

Fundamental to the RJKD practice of Reiki is mindfulness.
Mindfulness ultimately leads us to the realization of the Truth of
being. When we engage in any of the energy cultivation practices
we bring to bear the quality of mindfulness. Each of the processes
requires of the practitioner an engagement with the need to be
mindful. Mindful of the breath and of the consequent flow of
energy. Mindful of the body's posture at any given moment.
Mindful of the state of relaxation or tension that the body is in
and mindful of the sensations of energy flow in various points
as the practice is underway.  The exercises would be essentially
meaningless without this quality of mindfulness. All of the
exercises combine elements of movement and of stillness. In the
moving elements as the author Daniel Reid noted in his book *Chi
Gung, Harnessing the Power of the Universe* we seek 'stillness within
movement' and in the still elements we seek 'movement within
stillness', with the breath serving as the functional link between
these two aspects. When our mindfulness is highly developed and
we can bring this state of mental focus into our practice we are
also strengthening our formal meditation practice. The practice
helps us to apply wisdom in harnessing our passions. We are in
a sense using water to control fire and so our mindfulness/intent
manages the flow of energy rather than the energy being wasted
or misdirected by emotions. Importantly in the context of these
exercises, we are encouraging a strong and dynamic flow of *ki*/
Reiki through the body and thus helping to restore it to a state of
healthful balance. Of course mindfulness is a state that we also
wish to bring to our engagement with Reiki Therapeutics, and is

developed through our 'meditation with the hands' technique of using *The Six Point Meditation* in a hands-on context.

Mindfulness of the posture that we take when we engage in practice is also crucial. This is less so to a degree with the energy awareness/palm activation exercise taught at 2nd Degree as this can quite easily be done whilst sitting comfortably in an armchair, but certainly in *The Seven Purifying and Strengthening Breaths* and with the four 3rd Degree exercises, posture is critical. An ancient Chinese medical text noted that "When posture is not proper, energy is not smooth; when energy is not smooth, mind is not stable." When correct posture is adopted energy is drawn from the earth and its flow through the body is accelerated. At the same time this alignment creates the perfect conditions for Universal Energy (Reiki) to be channeled unhindered through the body's energetic system. We thus connect the two great forces of heaven and earth and fuse them together within. This is not to say that Reiki is a 'heavenly' energy only. Of course the energy that is drawn from the earth is also Reiki, but of a particular vibrational form that connects us to energy that has a strong resonance with our own state of physicality. Even minor deviations from the correct posture can affect the flow of energy as it travels through the body and this in turn can have a consequent effect on the stillness and state of equipoise of the mind. This is very much a Catch 22 situation however as the mind needs to be properly aligned at the start of practice for the energy to flow smoothly. If this is not the case then the posture can be influenced into a state of relative instability. For beginners it is much easier to take the proper posture, as near as is possible, than it is to focus and balance the mind, and so, this should be a primary concern at the start of practice.

As we assume our posture for the exercise we need to be aware that in connecting heaven and earth (drawing in Reiki from above and below) our *Tan Tien* acts as the central reservoir for this energy. Reiki may well be manifesting in the hands as is usual for a Reiki practitioner, but as we engage in abdominal breathing and certainly when we bring our focus to the *Tan Tien*, the Reiki energy intermingles with our own energy and accumulates at this point. This reservoir then acts like a pump sending the *chi/ki*/Reiki through the body's energy circuit. It travels down the legs to the feet and then back up the body to the arms and into the hands and then finally back up the arms and into the neck and head before returning to the *Tan Tien*. It is the natural Reiki flow following its normal course that ultimately manifests in the hands combined with the intensity of our own *chi* intermingled with Reiki once it has reached the hands that creates such an incredibly powerful focus of transmitted energy. As the body/arms move through the various changes in posture and muscle tensioning the pressure on the internal organs is reduced and induces energy to flow in greater abundance and with more force to the hands, and finally to the head before completing the circuit. It is our mental focus that helps to keep the energy intensity at the hands rather than it dissipating as the circuit back to the *Tan Tien* is completed.

In common with other energy-based disciplines the methods taught contribute to the overall health and wellbeing of the practitioner, either in maintaining it or restoring it after illness. Blockages or interruptions of the flow of vital energy within the body can cause either mental or physical imbalances. The body's network of energy channels acts like any other transportation system. When there is a blockage it will automatically overload the whole system. In the short term this can usually be compensated for in some way, but over time, serious and permanent damage can be done if the blockage is not dealt with. Through the adoption of specific body postures, focused intent and correct breathing practices which affect the movement of the energy, the energy cultivation exercises when used in tandem with regular Reiki self treatments, can address these blockages very quickly and restore the flow of energy to its optimum efficiency. As the energy travels throughout the system it nourished both internally and externally. As the channels open fully, energy flows freely and effortlessly. Amongst the many benefits of practice, blood pressure is reduced to a healthy state, the immune and circulatory systems are improved and the heart is strengthened by reducing its pulse. The deep, abdominal breathing that is used also helps to restore the bloods normal pH balance due to the effect of oxygenating the blood. At the same time the protective energy shield around the body is reinforced and enhanced. In this way, as we restore ourselves and the energy flows, we are able to pass on this energy in a variety of ways to others in an unhindered fashion as an expression of universal compassion to aid their journey back to healing into wholeness.

My own experience in engaging with these various methods is that they all have a powerfully invigorating effect on the whole body and mind. First thing in the morning, a few minutes of going through the moves of *The Seven Purifying and Strengthening Breaths* brings a strong sense of purpose and optimism to the day ahead as the body takes on a naturally healthy rhythm and energy flows abundantly. The mind feels clearer and sharper for the time taken to be focused mindfully. In practicing the four 3rd Degree exercises I find that the intensity of energy flow is astonishing. The tensing and releasing of the body with focused intent driving the flow of energy results in a dramatic build up of energy that can feel quite explosive and incredibly empowering. It is almost as if there is a storm of energy building within. Regular practice of these exercises results in a much increased feeling of emotional balance and vibrancy and brings a 'feel good' factor to every part of one's life. In engaging in these practices, there is a sense that, as *Qi Gong* Master Wang Xiang Zhai once noted:

> You are the sea. Whatever anyone gives you, you can take. They can also take from you anything they want. The sea is vast; it can give up anything and still remain the sea. Like the sea, you are endless and unceasing. This is true freedom.

# 10
# Symbols and Mantras

I searched for God and found only myself. I searched for myself and found only God.

*Sufi Proverb*

Symbols (or *shirushi* in Japanese) can be regarded as a midway point between the external physical existence and what is deeply embedded within. They are one of the ways in which we can approach the Divine essence within ourselves by internalizing our consciousness and allowing the inherent nature and purpose of the symbol to lead us to higher states of awareness. By using symbols we can raise our consciousness and so achieve enlightenment. All cultures and all spiritual and religious traditions use symbols. Symbolism seems to be somehow genetically coded into us. It is almost as if on some deep and primordial level we recognize that there is a need to connect with something that is fundamental and essential in our natures that is not immediately obvious and that is greater than our sense of individuality and the smallness of the lives that we live in the mundane world. So we use symbols

147

as a tool to make this connection – to tap into the mystery of life. They bind together and integrate these different orders of reality and so allow the possibility of realizing unity with the All. By holding a symbol as sacred, whether it is the Christian Cross, the Star of David, the Wheel of the Dharma or the Reiki symbols we imbue it with meaning and a power beyond the reckoning of our limited consciousness. The symbol takes on a life of its own through our awareness and transcends normal consciousness as it emanates essential qualities of the Universal Energy Field or God. These qualities, whilst imbued by the accessing mind, are also inherent as the imbuing mind or individual consciousness is accessing the Universal Energy Field and thus the innate qualities of the symbol that are an extension into physical form of the Universal Energy Field. By working with a symbol we can tap into the qualities that it represents and so access the eternal truths that are normally beyond the reach of everyday consciousness. However, the level of access that we gain is dependent upon the focus and ability of the accessing mind. The symbol acts as a filter for our consciousness.

As a part of sacred geometry and one of the universal archetypes through which energy is channeled, the Reiki symbols provide us with an excellent tool for focusing our energies simply by concentrating on them. When we understand the language of the symbols we have access to the spiritual truths that they represent. My Reiki Master, Gordon Bell, noted that "We must be aware that the symbol is a living and ever-expanding thing. It is a living organic entity which acts as a release-valve and transformer of psychic energy." So the symbol expresses an aspect of life and of the truth that once realized will lead beyond itself. It points to something bigger than that which is immediately apparent. It allows us access in a profound way to the energetic nature of the universe, and to transform higher vibrational frequencies or higher states of being into a form that is capable of manifestation in the physical realm of everyday experience. The symbol provides the key to manifestation of that which is un-manifest.

The question of where symbols come from is one that deserves attention. On one level of course they are created by human hand and mind. Had Christ been crucified on something other than a cross, then it is unlikely that the cross would have been used as a symbol to represent all that it now does for the Christian faith. Some other symbol would have been used. This explains only a small part of the creation of symbols, however. Symbols, whilst brought into the physical low vibration realm by the human mind (through our awareness) are in fact transcendent, living things that already exist within the depths of the subconscious and the Universal Energy Field. The energy of their emanation into physical form is already there, defined and precise, waiting for the mind of humanity to access it. The symbol does however need to be awakened by the mental concentration of the practitioner. The cross and the spiral are two good examples of this that although they differ in many minor aspects of their realized form, are shared by different cultures and different traditions over the millennia. These symbols were not physically carried from one place to another but accessed by the highly realized minds of practitioners within these different cultures and traditions. Symbols are in fact very much living things and are not dependent for their power or existence on a mind that needs to imbue it with meaning first. If this were not so, we could project onto any symbol any qualities or attributes that we like and thus the whole system of Reiki and symbolism in general becomes reduced to an act of faith. The mind can effect the specific orientation and level of vibration of the symbol for that particular mind when it is fully cognizant of the symbol's meaning and the methods of accessing it, but the symbol is independent of these requirements. The mind can give a symbol life, but this is a life that is tied to that particular mind or that particular mind's view of the power and attributes of the symbol based on the level of development of the consciousness at the time of access. Essentially, the power or qualities of the symbol are already out there, when we create a symbol to access those qualities we draw on universal attributes that are also out there and so the visual form is arrived at based on these universal attributes and our mind's ability to process this information and turn it into a concrete visual form. It is possible, for instance, to give someone a symbol on which to meditate without them having prior knowledge of what the symbol represents. Through diligent work with the symbol the meditator can uncover the meaning and power behind it on their own as the deep meditative states that they reach begin to access the level of truth within the Universal Energy Field that is represented by the symbol. The shape or 'look' of the symbol hides and so can reveal many complex ideas and an entire philosophy. Through distilling this information into a single symbolic form it gives the meditator something simple on which to focus their attention.

Fundamental to the mechanics of the Reiki symbols is something called *form energy* or *shape energy*. This is the concept that every shape emits a particular type of energy – energy of a specific vibration. It is a concept that every artist intuitively knows to be a critical and fundamental fact of the practice of their discipline. It is not just the shape created by the lines of the symbols that are important, but also the shape of the space around them and in between the component parts. All of these shapes carry a specific energetic quality that needs the particular and specific shape of the symbol to express it. There is no other form that will do exactly the same job. I have heard it said that the form of a symbol is relatively unimportant and that it is only the function with which we should concern ourselves. Without the form however, we cannot access the function. There are many famous examples of the use of specific shapes within the context of energy work. We can think of the Great Pyramids of Egypt as an example. Volumes have been written on the energetic qualities of pyramids when used with precisely defined and accurate measurements. The circle is another powerful shape – think of all of the standing stone circles across Europe. The Christian cross is yet another. These are all universal archetypal forms and there are many others. So when we meditate on the

Reiki symbols we are not working with some arbitrary shape that was simply 'thought up' to represent certain energetic qualities. There simply was no other form that could express those qualities in such a precise and definite way. The pure form however does not preclude stylistic nuances. Take for example an apple. The essence/energy of 'apple' is out there in the Universal Energy Field. When this essence manifests, it manifests as an apple – in all sorts of varieties, but always as an apple. It doesn't manifest as a rock or a cow or an orange. This energy must always express itself through a particular form with particular attributes. We get to know it when we eat it. The arrival of spiritual symbols in the world is due to a selfless act of revelation the type of which is the preserve of only the most highly realized spiritual masters.

A number of years ago following a 2nd Degree class, one of my students who was involved in charity work in Gambia came back to me following a visit to a remote village that was in desperate need of relief from grinding poverty and the consequent pervasive ill health that follows from poor living conditions and lack of food. The village that she visited had never before been visited by anyone from outside of its own culture. Whilst in the village this Reiki student had the opportunity to witness a healing being performed by the village healer/wise man. She was taken aback at one point during the process when she saw him carefully and precisely draw onto the body of the patient the Reiki Power symbol, whilst muttering something under his breath. This man cannot possibly have received Reiki training or any other form of training in healing outside of that which was passed down from his own ancestors. So how did he get to know the Reiki Power symbol? This symbol, like all universal truths, was and is already there, living and available via the Universal Energy Field of which we are all an emanation. It was his birthright as much as it is ours. Accessing symbols is not so much about gaining something new, but about waking up to something that we already know on a deep level. During my own 2nd Degree training after receiving the Reiki symbols I went to bed only to wake the next morning with the immediate realization that I had spent the whole night scrutinizing and laboring over the symbols in a very intense way. I was accessing a very deep part of myself that I had previously been unaware of. So spiritual symbols, not just Reiki symbols, exist already beyond our conscious awareness. They are alive and not merely dead forms waiting for a mind to give them life.

The Reiki symbols have been the most talked about, argued over and meddled with aspect of the entire Reiki system. Symbols are of course mystical, and people love anything mystical and so they have become a major preoccupation for many. The Reiki symbols however, like all other aspects of the system, are simply a set of tools, and are not something to be too strongly attached to. They are an extremely important aspect of the system and it would be difficult to perform the Reiki attunements without them, but on the spiritual path we need to learn to let go of our attachments, and this ultimately includes the Reiki symbols. Whilst we need these tools however, we should use them with care and with a sense of their sacredness and with an awareness of their true purpose and meaning. Having said this there are many within the Reiki community that suggest that once sufficient practice with the symbols has been done, there is no longer a need to continue working with them as we develop the ability to tune into their primary functions on almost a subconscious level. This is only partly true. Experience will certainly show that it is possible for instance to make a direct connection for the purposes of distant healing without the need to laboriously draw and invoke the Distant or Absent symbol every time as this particular function of the symbol becomes deeply embedded within us. However, in relinquishing our use of the symbols at this stage of development is to miss the opportunity to explore the full depths of their meaning and function. In staying with the Distant symbol as an example, it has many, many more attributes beyond its apparent singular function in connecting us energetically to another person. Mastery of the symbol is required. Being able to do distant healing without consciously invoking Symbol 3 or increasing energy flow without consciously invoking Symbol 1 is not Mastery in any meaning of the word, but a first step along the path. It would be foolish to stop working with the Reiki symbols at such an early stage of development within this energy-based discipline.

In RJKD the four traditional Reiki symbols are taught. They are basically the same symbols that are taught in other Reiki lineages, though their form differs slightly in a number of ways. This form does not change from one Master of the lineage to another or from one generation of Masters to another. It is important that the symbols remain in their true and original form and so students are generally given hard copies of the symbols and encouraged to learn how to draw them accurately. This is important. Whilst the third and fourth symbols are Japanese *kanji* and in some senses can therefore be open to stylistic nuance, the first two symbols are based on the original Tibetan/Sanskrit symbols taught within the *Buddho-EnerSense* system. So deviation from the true form, whilst still providing an energetic connection with the internal meaning of the symbols (through the conscious intent of the practitioner), can over time and as the deviations evolve, weaken the energetic connection to the true form of the symbols within the *Buddho-EnerSense* system. In RJKD, in line with the general convention, the symbols are known either by their equivalent mantra qualities (names) or simply as Symbol 1, Symbol 2, etc.

I think that it is important to make clear at this point that there is no hard and fast evidence to suggest that Mikao Usui discovered the Reiki symbols within the *Buddho-EnerSense* system. We do know that he had the first three cycles of the *Buddho* meditation and so it is possible that during his meditative retreat on Mt Kurama that he accessed the form of at least one of the symbols through this practice. However it is also possible that he accessed the symbols (the roots of which are all contained within the *Buddho-EnerSense* system) from some other source. It would appear however that given Usui's knowledge of the *Buddho* meditation, and possibly other material within the system, that he may well have arrived at the symbols from working with material

that could have been either the *Buddho-EnerSense* system itself (or
a part of it) or material of a similar nature. Whatever the truth,
it is interesting to note that the four symbols passed on by Usui
are identical to the four Reiki symbols that are derivatives of the
mantras and yantras of *Buddho-EnerSense*. There is a connection
between Sanskrit and some of the Reiki symbols, and there are
also references back to Chinese, Tibetan and Japanese Buddhism,
but none of the symbols can be traced to a single letter of the
Sanskrit alphabet. What is clear is that with the Reiki symbols we
have a direct connection back to not only Mikao Usui but also to
Buddhist practice and thus to the Buddha. This is an important
point because it answers the question of why would Usui use a
set of symbols that simply replaced other 'symbols'? The Reiki
symbols are non-denominational, and do not require of the
practitioner any engagement with Buddhist ideas or practices and
thus they are in a sense symbolic of the skillful means which Usui
employed in developing his entire system of non-denominational
Reiki or *Usui Do*.

It has been suggested that Usui introduced the symbols at
the time that Chujiro Hayashi and the other naval officers were
receiving their training from him to provide them with tools that
they could use to help them feel the Reiki energy as they were
not particularly sensitive to it. It is unlikely that the symbols were
introduced into the system – at whatever point this happened
(which was almost certainly very much prior to the arrival of
the naval officers) – simply to increase sensitivity to energy flow.
Increasing sensitivity may be the direct result of implementing
the symbols in Reiki practice, but it is not their only purpose.
They hide profound and complex truths and given the spiritual/
philosophical nature of Usui's original *Usui Do* system it is more
likely that they were introduced as a tool to help students on
their own path to self-knowledge. It may be the case that as
Hayashi was very much focused on the healing aspects of Reiki
that Usui passed them on to him and his colleagues principally
for this purpose and that Hayashi then passed on the symbols

himself without elaborating on much more of their use and value beyond that which is applicable to the healing process (sensitivity to energy being one aspect). The Reiki symbols are a part of the core of the system to help in the exploration of its fundamental truths and not just an 'add on' or an afterthought.

There has been much debate over whether or not the names of the symbols are indeed names at all or whether in fact they are separate mantric devices that are simply associated with the visual representations that call upon the same energetic qualities. In RJKD the names of the symbols are used as a mantra (*jumon* or *kotodama* in Japanese) to aid the focus of the practitioner in activating and realizing the qualities and potentialities of the symbol. Each symbol has a symbolic (visual) form and a mantric form. For Symbols 3 and 4 the sounds (names) are the mantra and the *kanji* (Japanese script) is the written form of the sounds that form the symbol. From the point of view of *Buddho-EnerSense*, each of the Reiki symbols has a mantra and yantra (visual meditation device) associated with it and from which it is derived and these are typically of Buddhist or Sanskrit origin. The symbols are derived from the yantra and the name is the Japanese description or version of the mantra. Had Usui spoken English instead of Japanese then the mantra/name and associated qualities and functions of the symbols would have been expressed through English. The Japanese description that we have invokes the same qualities and energies as the original mantra that it is based on. This requires of the practitioner a focus on the spiritual aspects of the Japanese mantra — they have other associations that are not necessarily spiritual. For instance the name of the Power symbol (Symbol 1) if one does an internet search is seen to be used in a variety of non-spiritual contexts. It is well recognized that the name of this symbol essentially means 'imperial command' and in this context it can be found as a description of a number of imperial commands that relate to various edicts of Japanese emperors. So whilst the name of a Reiki symbol can be used in a mantric form, they do have other associations that are non-spiritual. By using the Japanese name/mantra for the symbols we connect to the same qualities that are called upon by the original Buddhist/Sanskrit mantras that they relate to and which are inherent within the Universal Energy Field. When we draw the symbol or invoke the name/mantra for the symbol we connect this quality. As Ranga noted "We are creating a state of consciousness that is in resonance with the symbol (or mantra)." In RJKD the mantra and the symbol are used together as mutually supportive devices, however they can and are used independently of each other. In the *Buddho-EnerSense* system it is a common practice to work with mantra. This practice was given to me as a part of my Reiki training also. This may not be a universal practice amongst teachers of RJKD, but it is a logical extrapolation of practices within *Buddho-EnerSense* and can be usefully applied in the context of Reiki. So the names of the symbols can be used as a mantra, independent of the symbols to invoke the associated qualities of the Universal Energy Field. However, since yantra and mantra are complementary aspects of the same force, it is much more efficient to use them together.

It has been claimed that it is possible to activate the Reiki symbols simply by thinking or voicing its associated number. I see no reason for this not to be the case as the number relates to the body of information about the symbol within the mind of the practitioner. However, this is a simplistic method of accessing only the symbol's apparent external function of connecting to the energy type represented by the symbol. It cannot access the full depths of the symbol in the same way as intoning, internally or externally, the mantric name of the symbol or from visualizing/drawing the symbol itself.

When we receive the Reiki attunements, the symbols — form and meaning — are integrated into our energy fields through the focused intent of the initiating Reiki Master. They become a part of our own energetic makeup or blueprint. This happens during the 1st Degree attunements to form the connection to the stream of Reiki energy even though we will not receive the symbols themselves until we train at 2nd Degree. Having taken the 2nd Degree we are then able to use the symbols to focus energy, in much the same way that a magnifying glass focuses light from the sun, and this enables us to concentrate or direct Reiki in certain ways. When we work with the symbols either through visualization, or through drawing them, or in repeating the associated mantra, we can access their inherently high vibrational state, their imprint in the Universal Energy Field, as we raise our own consciousness. Our minds are a tremendous source of creative power. In fact, at the time of accessing this level of vibration, we 'become' the symbol that we are working with – our resonance is the same. In visualizing or working with the symbol/energy we create within the Universal Energy Field the symbol itself and also match our own vibration to that which is already an integral part of the Universal Energy Field. The Creator and the created become one and so there is no beginning or end. The symbol in representing the union of microcosm and macrocosm both precedes and follows the act of visualization. It is very much a chicken and egg situation!

In RJKD, partly as a consequence of the fact that the lineage has been carried by very advanced practitioners who were all Japanese speaking up until 1990, and partly due to the origination material on the symbols/mantras that is a part of the *Buddho-EnerSense* system being held within the lineage, their energetic function and mechanism is taught to a depth that would not be possible without reference to the original Sanskrit/Tibetan material. The Reiki symbols are a simplified form of the original Buddhist material and therefore in exploring the depths of these symbols we only invoke some of the qualities associated with the original material. The Reiki symbols however do have many levels of meaning. Intellectual knowledge, whilst needing to be developed as much as possible, does not automatically give rise to the ability to access the depth of the qualities available to us. Along with this knowledge we need to integrate into our lives regular study and practice along with meditation over a sustained period of time to activate the deeper attributes of the symbols. The possibilities for using the symbols are limited only by the practitioner's imagination. The dual role of the Reiki symbols as a tool for self-exploration and as an aid to the practice of Reiki Therapeutics very much echoes the entire philosophic orientation of the Reiki system.

✳

The names/mantras for the Reiki symbols are not given below, but are instead referred to numerically and by their associated commonly known primary qualities and functions. I have restricted myself to discussing the principle and widely known attributes of the symbols and not the many ways in which they can be used. This information is easily accessible via Reiki classes and through many Reiki books and the internet. As with other lineages and traditions in Reiki, the first three symbols are taught at 2nd Degree and the final symbol is taught as a part of the 3rd Degree or Masters level training. Within RJKD, at Masters level the *kanji* form of the first two symbols is also taught.

In applying the Reiki symbols to external physical reality we place them (or 'intend' them) on or over the object, person or situation that we wish to see transformed by the specific qualities of the symbol, and then invoke the mantric form of the symbol to boost the connection. This process can be done as an entirely internal exercise with no proximal or visual connection to the receiver of the energy, or done physically in the presence of the recipient – either way works as well as the other.

## Symbol 1 (The Power Symbol)

The Power symbol and mantric name are the principle symbolic tools of the Reiki system. The essential meaning of these tools is 'imperial spirit' or 'imperial command' (or 'edict'). When we utilize these devices we are saying 'put the power of the Universe here' and we are accessing the primary energetic nature of all that is. It acts like the command of God and bypasses or eliminates all obstacles in its path (hence its use by some to create a parking space, or get other traffic out of the way when in a hurry!). It not only activates and increases the flow of Reiki energy within us, and connects the physical realm of existence to the immaterial realm of Spirit but focuses the energy for particular conscious intent. It expresses both male and female energy and the rising of the *kundalini* life force. Some have suggested that the association of the Power Symbol with the *kundalini* life force is an untenable cultural jump from Japan to India. This is not so. The symbols derive from Buddhism, and Buddhism was born in India. The system of *Buddho-EnerSense* which gives us the Power Symbol derives much from the Indian spiritual tradition.

This symbol/mantra, which exists beyond the normal concepts of time and space can be used in isolation, or in conjunction with the other Reiki symbols/mantras to increase or magnify the vibratory rate of the qualities that they represent by bringing to bear the qualities of supreme enlightenment. It can also be used to help protect and to pass on a blessing. It is multi-functional and the potentiality of its power is truly awesome, being limited only by the imagination and commitment to practice of the Reiki student. It is the key to the whole Reiki system and due to that which it represents is common to all life, and as such is therefore accessible to all – including village healers in Gambia!

## Symbol 2 (The Mental/Emotional Symbol)

There seems to be a growing momentum behind 'factualizing' the assumption that this symbol is derived simply from the Sanskrit character *hrih* or *kiriku* in Japanese in spite of the lack of evidence for this beyond their visual similarity and the association of the seed syllable *hrih* with the deity Amitabha (the Buddha of Limitless Light). Symbol 2 has its origins in the Sanskrit language but is not derived from any one single Sanskrit character as is commonly believed. The function of Symbol 2 is to instill a state of tranquility within the mind of the practitioner, bringing it back to its natural state of harmony by balancing the left and right hemispheres of the brain – the logical and intellectual side with the intuitive and creative side. In its function as a mechanism for restoring balance it also brings about a state of equilibrium between the conscious and subconscious minds and as such it is often referred to as 'humanity and God becoming One'. The fundamental qualities of this symbol express a powerful and dynamic creativity that allows for the recreation of Creation within every moment. All areas of life, including the physical and energetic systems of the body and mind, can be restored to a state of harmonious symmetry with the use of this symbol. It can be used to restore peace to many situations in our day-to-day lives. Thus it is used to work on all manner of mental/emotional issues and problems including anxiety, stress, depression and fear. As the Buddha pointed out, our minds and thus our lives are constantly going out of balance as we form attachments that weigh us down and skew our vision of the true state of being. By using this symbol we can connect to causes and so restore the natural balance of things. Some practitioners also use this symbol to help with memory recall and for programming in positive mental and emotional habits and responses to the events in their lives as it works directly on the subconscious level.

In working with this symbol/mantra as we bring our minds back to a state of natural harmony we are able to use this tool as a way of beginning to unravel the causes and effects of our propensity to create attachments in our lives that result in continued suffering. We can use it to undermine our illusory self-images based on ego-driven needs to be right, perfect, in control and totally self-sufficient. We can find what it is that we truly need in our lives by allowing negative thought patterns to dissolve and be replaced by positive life-enhancing ones, and thus restore a state of optimum physical and mental health.

# Symbol 3 (The Absent or Distant Symbol)

This symbol and Symbol 4 are not so much symbols in and of themselves but the Japanese written version of the mantra that expresses the qualities of particular yantras within the Buddhist canon and that are found within the *Buddho-EnerSense* system. However, in the manner in which they are written, they form a symbolic device that allows for the exploration of the internal meanings of the original source material in a multiplicity of ways. With Symbol 3 for instance it was a common practice for Seiji Takamori to contemplate the various syllable components that form the symbol in different ordering combinations, thus revealing further depths of meaning. Since the *kanji* of this symbol is fused together, the concepts and information that it represents are also interrelated. The mantric name of Symbol 3 has been translated to mean in general terms as 'wholeness', implying that when used it gets in touch with the whole being or ground of being. This is only a small part of a symbol that is replete with many interwoven threads of meaning.

Symbol 3 is often called the Distant or Absent Symbol as it is primarily used in the practice of distant healing. However, since the connection to people, things and events over distance (and also time) is a principle characteristic of this tool, it is also possible to use it to connect to other levels of being that are not a part of the physical realm – perhaps to those who have left the physical plain of existence or to connect to past life issues. Generally speaking, by using Symbol 3 we call in the participation of other spiritual beings and connect to the essential nature or God Consciousness within ourselves or another, and this is what we do whenever we use the symbol.

# Symbol 4 (The Master Symbol)

The Master symbol is used principally for attuning others into the system of Reiki by allowing the initiating Master to transmit an immense amount of energy for activating the *chakras* and energy channels or *nadis* to a much higher level. It is a symbol therefore that should only be shared with Reiki Masters. When used in the attunement process, the inherent truths and energetic qualities of the originating mantra from which this symbol is derived are imprinted permanently into the energy field of the student. Once the seed is sown it is then up to the student to realize the potential that this symbol represents. Its name/mantric form is often translated as 'Great Bright Light' or 'The Great Ray of Enlightenment'. It has been said that this symbol encapsulates the very essence of the Reiki experience and combines the energies of the other three symbols on a much more subtle level. Whether this is true or not, it does not suggest as some have claimed, that once mastered, the other three symbols can be dispensed with. This would be to profoundly limit the potentiality of the Reiki system to provide the practitioner with opportunities for further growth and development.

It is believed that this symbol works at the cellular and genetic level and can be used to bring about clarity of purpose in revealing an individual's true purpose in life, often leading to dramatic changes in career and lifestyle. It is also believed that Symbol 4 also increases intuitive and psychic awareness, though sustained work with any of the symbols will actually lead one along this path.

✳

Of the many ways that the Reiki symbols can be used I have focused briefly on what are for me the two primary methods of accessing the deeper qualities and potentialities of the symbols: meditation and mantra recitation. Both practices are developed within RJKD, though there is more of an emphasis given to the meditation aspect within the lineage. Since all of our problems ultimately stem from the mind, in developing a sense of inner and outer peace and harmony, it is to our minds that we need to address our efforts. As our practice of meditation and mantra recitation with these forms develops we find that our attachments to worldly distractions dissolve and our innate qualities of compassion and wisdom become magnified.

# Meditation

All of the Reiki symbols are excellent material to work with as another focus for *Samatha* (and *Vipassana*) meditation and RJKD students are encouraged to engage in this practice. There are many ways of working with the symbols in this context, but principally the two main ways are with an internal focus or with an external focus. They can either be visualized and held within the mind, or drawn onto a piece of card and the eyes allowed to rest on the form. Combinations are also possible, for instance drawing out the symbol onto card first, absorbing the symbol visually and then internalizing it. In the beginning of this type of internalizing practice, it easiest to simply hold the image of the symbol at the third eye – this is where we visualize. As practice develops the symbol can be held at other points on the body or within the various energy centers and channels of the body. When we do this, the energetic nature of the symbol is localized and focused at the point on which we are holding the symbol, leading to a transmutation in our own energy state and so achieving balance and harmony at this point as energy flows. When we use this type of practice to bring the energy into the central channel (in Sanskrit known as *avadhuti*), which is located in front of the spine, the energy is able to influence the *chakras* located along its length and this results in a very deep level of concentration. When we then meditate on *shunyata* ('emptiness' or the interrelationship of everything) whilst in this state, it is claimed that we can achieve enlightenment very quickly.

As a meditative device the Reiki symbols work in the same way as the yantras from which they are derived. Yantras (which means 'support' or 'instrument') are generally geometric designs that contain specific spiritual significance that pertains to a higher level of consciousness. They are like microcosmic pictures of the macrocosm. Whether we use a traditional yantra or a Reiki Symbol as the object of meditation we bring our minds to a focus on a window to the Absolute. We focus on specific qualities or vibrational states of the Universal Energy Field. When we establish this state of resonance with the symbol by having a mental focus on it, energy flows. Eventually as our practice deepens over time we can reach a point of non-duality in which we can no longer tell whether the symbol is within us or we are within the symbol – the distinction between object and viewer becomes redundant. As we reach this deep absorptive state our senses no longer register external stimuli such as our surroundings or potentially distracting noises. In the same way that we become one with the object of our meditation in for instance *The Six Point Meditation*, so we do in meditating on the Reiki symbols. A state of *samadhi* or ecstasy is reached.

## Mantra

A mantra is a syllable or phrase that is repeated over and over again and which has some spiritual significance. The use of mantra can be found in many religious and spiritual traditions but is thought to have first been used within Hinduism, in which it has a pivotal role. The word 'mantra' is derived from Sanskrit and means 'to think' or 'that which protects the mind'. Mantras can have devotional significance but are also used as a meditative device for developing concentration or one-pointedness. They can be chanted out loud or internalized. Mantras are said to be 'sound symbols' and so carry the same meaning and function in invoking spiritual forces that are contained within the visual representation of the meanings and functions – the symbol. When we repeat a mantra, as when we draw or visualize a symbol, we align ourselves and identify with the particular spiritual quality that is represented by the sound/symbol. Within the human system, speech is the most direct and powerful expression of energy, which is why mantra has such a central role in Tibetan Buddhism. This is also recognized within Taoism where the healing aspects of *Qi Gong* are expressed through the use of sound in the *Six Syllable Secret* practice. Particular tones are also used to activate and harmonize the various *chakras* of the energy system. The practice of mantra or mantra meditation as an object of concentration can help to still the mind. Whilst the recitation of a mantra occupies the mind, there tends to be a natural decrease in distracting mental chatter, and so the mind is able to find its natural state of stillness and balance more easily. Even when there is a parallel stream of internal dialogue going on, the chanting of a mantra can create a sense of continuity and focus that will become the dominant force within the mind with continued practice. It is a bit like focusing on the ticking of a clock. As we focus more and more on the sound, we become more and more oblivious of other distracting sounds that are calling for our attention.

Mantra is a further tool that enhances one's ability in exploring Reiki fully. In the context of this discipline, a mantra might consist of the repetition of all of the names of the symbols strung together or the repetition of a single symbol name or any combination of the names, depending on the energetic focus of the practice. The important thing in mantra practice, like other energy disciplines, is to do it as often as possible. In working with mantra there is less excuse for not doing it than pretty much any other aspect of the system as it can be something that we engage in at any time of the day regardless of what we are doing. It needs to become an integral part of our internal discourse at all times. When we achieve this state it is possible to have other thoughts that relate to something that we need to give our immediate attention to whilst the mantra still continues 'in the background'. The use of mantra, like the use of meditation and self-treatment with Reiki will have a beneficial effect on your mental wellbeing. It can be incorporated very easily into all other Reiki practices, whether it is *The Six Point Meditation* or giving someone a hands-on treatment. I always use mantra during and immediately following the drawing of the Reiki symbols. It seems to empower and add a further boost to the energy.

✳

The power of the Reiki symbols and mantras is astonishing. They are not simple patterns and sounds that somehow through some mysterious process connect us to energies that we can use to help in the healing process. Of course they do this, and this is a wonderful expression of the quality of compassion, but they can also be used in the pursuit of our own liberation from endless rounds of suffering and to achieve the ultimate in healing – the attainment of *nibbana*. If as a Reiki practitioner you have dispensed with these 'training wheels' because you have learnt to 'switch on' their primary energetic functions without them, you would be well advised to pick them up again and perhaps explore them more fully.

# 11

# Reiki Therapeutics

Healing may not be so much about getting better, as about letting go of everything that isn't you – all of the expectations, all of the beliefs – and becoming who you are.

*Rachel Naomi Remen*

In considering the practice of Reiki therapeutics we are in some senses coming full circle. It is the use of Reiki as a therapeutic modality that it is most commonly known for and most of us during and following our 1st Degree class are anxious to try out our new found abilities as channels for healing energy. As we progress with our practice of Reiki within RJKD and through the levels of training a realization starts to emerge of the vastness of the Reiki system as a method for personal liberation and freedom. So, whilst still honoring the fundamental requirements of the Reiki canon to bring healing to others as often as we can, we begin a much more direct engagement with our own salvation through applying the methods that we have touched upon previously in this book for our own benefit. Eventually, as we break down our shackles, and feel the freedom that we have granted to ourselves, we develop a strong and profound desire to bring this feeling and sense of freedom to others, to relieve their suffering in whatever form that it may manifest, and contribute as much as we are able to creating a more just and 'lighter' world for everyone to live and love in. More than this however, we are able to bring to bear our own emerging wisdom mind, so that our efforts, even though at times small and outwardly of little consequence, can bear the most luxurious fruit. Each seed that we sow, if planted with the right intention and nurtured in the right way, can bring forth a forest of abundant healing for many, many people. So whilst the application of Reiki in a therapeutic setting is in some senses, the least of the system, it is in many ways an aspect of our ultimate goal. By developing our own wisdom minds and thus promoting universal compassion within ourselves, we then have the strong desire to turn outwards and bring this compassion to bear in a direct and immediate way for the relief of the suffering of others. What more natural expression of this is there for someone imbued with the gift of Reiki, than through the laying on of hands in a healing context?

It is worth emphasizing again how absolutely vital is the development of our own wisdom mind in this process, however. There is no greater goal than our own salvation, as we cannot be all that we can possibly be without great wisdom and thus great compassion. This is so critical to the healing process, not only for ourselves, but also for those others that we might be called upon to work with in our roles as channels for Reiki. We know that we cannot heal everyone and we learn that true healing can take many forms, and so we develop the wisdom to let go of our desires to achieve specific outcomes. People get ill and people die, and we are all going to die at some point from something. This is simply the way that it is meant to be and there is nothing that we can do about it. If we can accept this, then we can grasp it with the same enthusiasm that we grasp a new flower to inhale its fragrance. All of life, including death, is a wonderful opportunity for growth and creative, enthusiastic expression. If we can approach our own lives in this way, by turning every event, every mishap, every one of the slings and arrows of misfortune into the most precious jewel that we have ever seen, we entrench within us the most tremendous courage and strength to face life as it comes along and to help others face life in the same spirit. This is not to force upon others that which we believe to be the correct and proper way of things. Our egos are fundamentally out of synch with reality, and are no guide whatsoever upon which to base any judgment of anything. So we let go of the ego's predisposition to judge and apportion blame and its efforts to try to mold the world in its image and we begin to engage with all that is and learn to accept that we can be a channel for the ultimate expression of the truth as we lay our hands upon the suffering body of another being.

The practice of Reiki therapeutics within RJKD marks our connection to and practice of a style of Reiki that was principally pioneered by Chujiro Hayashi. It is a tradition that, like those in the Takata and the other Hayashi lineages, we are immensely proud of. In applying Reiki in a therapeutic setting we are in so many ways fulfilling the promise of the Reiki attunements that we received, and the admonitions of the Reiki Principles to express universal compassion for all other beings.

One very important part of engaging with the treatment aspect of the system within RJKD is the need, as was discussed earlier, to be very mindful of the way that we conduct the treatment process itself. In RJKD we aim to develop the mind of meditation through our concentration and awareness during the treatment process – the mind needs to be free and simply there in the moment. In developing this quality we may practice our *Six Point Meditation*. This can be the case during a self-treatment as much as when working with another person. In applying mindfulness and using the process as a form of meditation with the hands we gradually and by degrees remove our ego-centered self from the equation. This allows the energy to flow much more freely and thus to effect a deeper and more lasting state of balance and health than would otherwise be possible. It is very important within this tradition to bring a sense of mindfulness and sensitivity to the flow of energy in all treatments – each treatment that we conduct, on ourselves or another, is another step towards liberation. What is not appropriate when working on others, and which seems to be all too common a practice, is to become involved in a lengthy conversation with the recipient or to gaze around the room aimlessly during the treatment process itself. This reduces the recipient's ability to relax fully as the mind is engaged in dealing with the information that you are giving to it, and so the body cannot fully relax either. This way of conducting yourself also means that you inhibit your ability to channel the energy due to being ego-focused, and thus are then also inhibiting the ability of the recipient to draw the energy that they need in as beneficial a way as is possible. The treatment therefore is very much less than it could otherwise be. It is as important for the Reiki channel as it is for the recipient receiving the treatment to learn and grow with Reiki. A quiet, meditative approach to treatment is the most preferable.

Within RJKD there is a strong emphasis on working with the *chakra* system to bring balance to all areas of the body and mind. These *chakras*, as we have seen are related to the major functions of the body, mind and spirit and are our connection to the primordial flow of energy from the Universal Energy Field. As such it is clearly the case that an energetic healing system like Reiki must in some ways address this energetic map within and without the physical body. By placing the hands in line with or near to the *chakras*, energy flows and brings a state of equilibrium to the particular *chakra* which then in turn influences those aspects of the body and mind to which it is related. It distributes the Universal Energy through the *nadis* to all aspects and levels of being. If we are to work with the *chakras* in this way, then we need to develop our sensitivity to the flow of energy as much as possible, particularly in our hands, and this can be done not only through the various lineage methods previously described that are designed for this purpose but also through our work in treating ourselves with Reiki. In this way as our sensitivity increases we are able to sense the various fluctuations of energy in the *chakras* of others when we come to work on them.

It is very much the case however, and this has been emphasized by many Reiki practitioners in other publications, that the hand positions that are taught, whether for working on oneself or another, are very much a foundation from which to begin one's own search for a personal way of working. The methods taught, whilst covering all of the major parts of the physical and energetic bodies, are essentially rigid formats for treatment. This of course is an excellent way of introducing a practice to a newcomer, but as experience is accrued, it is necessary to develop a style and approach that is a little more intuitive, but without abandoning the taught foundation practice altogether. A keen insight is developed into how to approach each individual treatment as the energy guides the mind and hands of the practitioner. Of course if you are deeply entrenched in a conversation with the recipient then it is probably wise to stay with the rigid foundation protocol as you will not be able to respond to the guidance of the energy in any meaningful way.

## Self-treatment

The fundamental practice of the lineage, as one would expect, and in line with the traditions of the other Hayashi lineages, is that of self-treatment. It is vital to engage with this process more than any other and to apply Reiki in our own lives every single day. The Reiki attunements induce a rapid detoxification process that clears the mind and the body of all that is not conducive to a state of harmonious health and balance. This practice is not something that we do just for a few days or a couple of months – it is a lifetime's work. Just being within this physical existence means that we continually accrue imbalances on a physical and emotional level all of the time, and as each day passes, there is more detritus to clear. Self-treatment with Reiki should become as much a daily habit as brushing one's teeth or combing one's hair. If we persist long enough, then we raise our own vibrations and slowly but surely move out of resonance with those aspects of life that are not conducive to mental and physical peace. Life gets easier and flows more abundantly.

Within the RJKD tradition there have been at times different approaches to the practice of self-treatment. During my training at 1st Degree the style of working was very much reminiscent of the Hayashi/Takata model and concentrated primarily on bringing the Reiki energy to bear on the physical body with an emphasis on treating not only the seven major *chakras* but all of the major organs of the body and the endocrine glands. At 2nd Degree, there was a somewhat different approach to self- treatment and this was based on a model that was used and passed on to Ranga by Seiji Takamori. It is of course empowered by the use of the Reiki symbols, but focuses not just on the *chakra* system within the body, but also the aura surrounding the body and has an emphasis on bringing the whole energy field, which includes the *charkas,* back into a state of perfect alignment. There has however been some re-adjustment of the way that this process is now taught, and a common method has been introduced by Ranga at 1st and 2nd Degree, but with the addition of acu-points at 2nd Degree. At 3rd Degree, the self- treatment method alters, and includes the application of pressure to further acupressure points on the body with focused awareness of the energy flow through the *meridians.* The use of point work in these methods is a style of working that again is influenced by the larger system of *Buddho-EnerSense.*

In applying Reiki through these points we bring the energy to bear directly to specific organs and other parts of the body/mind to which the points are related, and increase the natural flow of bodily energy that circulates through the associated *nadis*. The result of this is that we are much more able to achieve a deeply penetrative exposure of the whole being to a very intense and focused energy flow.

# Treating Others

There are different approaches to the treatment of other people contained within the RJKD canon. At 1st Degree I was taught a method of working using a treatment table that is very much reminiscent of the approach handed down to us from Chujiro Hayashi, and would be recognized by most within the Reiki community at large. However we do have other protocols for engaging in this process of working on or with others.

Two different approaches to giving a seated treatment are developed, one at 1st Degree and another at 2nd Degree. The 1st Degree approach is very much concerned with bringing the *chakras* back into alignment as quickly as possible and is a relatively quick treatment, ideal for when time is short, or for use in emergency situations. The 2nd Degree seated treatment, which again is quite a quick process, was a method employed by Seiji Takamori and passed on to Ranga. In carrying out this method of treatment, the practitioner focuses much more on working with the energy field around the body and 'tuning in' to the fluctuations and energetic imbalances within this area, whilst also guiding the recipient's awareness to those areas and imbalances as they are being worked upon. From my own experience I would say that this is a deeply penetrative treatment protocol and maximizes the opportunity for the practitioner to really engage on an incredibly profound level with the nature of the individual's energy field and with the Universal Energy Field of which the individual is a part, thus blurring and then eliminating the distinction between giver and receiver. The sense of unity or one-ness with the recipient that the practitioner can experience during this process is one that for me really defies description in any meaningful way and simply needs to be experienced.

As with other traditions in Reiki, RJKD also makes use of treatment protocols that involve the recipient being prone on a treatment table or bed. Within this lineage there is a distinctly different approach to this process than one might find elsewhere within the Reiki community. As mentioned previously, reports do seem to be emerging that Usui used a method that involved the application of pressure to specific points on the body. This is a method that was introduced to the Reiki canon within RJKD by Ranga, who extracted the philosophical basis of this approach from the larger teaching of *Buddho-EnerSense* in creating a specific approach that is suitable as a Reiki method.

The method introduced in a basic way at 1st Degree and then developed further at 2nd and 3rd Degree combines a multiplicity of approaches. Whilst there is extensive use of the hands-on approach to treat the *chakras* and *nadis,* there is also a great emphasis on working with the recipient's energy field, again with a focus on bringing awareness to the fluctuations of energy within this area, and also in applying pressure to specific *marma* points (or vital energy points) on the body, many of which correspond to particular acupressure points (*tsubos*). This approach to treatment balances the *chakras* and *nadis* and energizes the *marma* points as well as the *meridians*, which are used so extensively within Traditional Chinese Medicine. The treatment is enhanced by bringing the recipient's focused awareness to the points and channels being treated, as this also aids in the movement of energy.

Through the external stimulation of Reiki energy, the effect of this approach is to encourage energy to leap from one point to another, or one pathway to another, within the internal energy matrix and this in turn sets up a series of modified, temporary flows of energy that balance the whole system. This energizing of the whole body's circuitry can be a very intense experience for many people and lead to deep and profound healing on many levels. As with the use of *marma* point work during self-treatment, we bring the energy to bear very quickly and efficiently on those aspects of the body that are related to the particular points that are treated.   Since the use of *marma* points is a fundamental practice within RJKD it is worth reflecting on the theoretical and philosophical basis of their use a little further.

# Marma Shastra

*Marma Shastra* is the name of the ancient Indian martial art from which the art of *Marma Adi* is derived. It is a part of the larger therapeutic discipline of *Ayurveda* whose history can be traced back 7000 years to the civilizations of ancient India. *Marma Adi* is the practice of manipulating *marmas* which are found close to the skin to effect healing and is the most revered of Indian healing systems. The striking or massaging of these nerve junctures can produce either healing or deleterious results through the manipulation of the flow of vital energy, and in this respect, at least as far as healing is concerned, the practice has a great deal in common with the Chinese practice of acupressure. There are some differences, however. In the Chinese system there are considered to be 14 *meridians* with 361 *tsubo* or *marma* points. In the *Ayurvedic* system of *Marma Shastra/Adi* there are thought to be 26 *meridians* in all, 12 of which are located in pairs on the left and right sides. There are thousands of *marma* points on the body, 365 of which are considered to be of the most significance. According to the ancient Indian *Kalari* system there are 64 critical *marma* points, however the author Susruta in his *Ayurvedic* classic *Susruta Samhita* lists 107 'lethal *marmas*'. These points which are said to be where life is maintained, if damaged can give rise to extreme pain, unconsciousness or death. In terms of the practices within RJKD however, only a small fraction of this total are used. The *marma* points boost the energy/*chi*/*ki*/*prana* each time it flows through, which results in a much-enhanced level of life force energy for the individual. This flow varies in intensity depending on the time of day as it peaks and diminishes following a 24-hour cycle. Precision in the use of *marma* points according to the classic *Ayurvedic* approach is crucial, and can take many years of training, however in the application of Reiki to these points we have the benefit of knowing that Reiki flows to where it is needed and is guided by the intensity of the practitioner's focus as well as the physical pressure applied to the points.

## Absent Treatment

The methods of conducting a distant or absent treatment within our lineage are broadly the same as those passed on by Hawayo Takata, which she learnt, as did Sensei Takeuchi, from Chujiro Hayashi. The RJKD approach does require mindfulness and an expectation that the Reiki channel will work, to a degree at least with the mantric aspects of the symbols that may be used within the treatment, as well as perhaps involvement in the practice of *The Six Point Meditation*.

A question that arises over and over again in relation to the Absent Treatment method is whether or not it is necessary to seek the permission of the recipient before Reiki is sent to them. There is within this question an inherent confusion and lack of understanding of the nature of the flow of Reiki energy. Reiki energy is not sent, it is drawn. When we open the channel for Reiki to flow, and, through invoking the Reiki symbols, connect to another at a distance, we are simply providing a channel through which the recipient can draw the energy, in the same way that is done during a hands-on treatment. So, regardless of what the individual might believe or voice about the prospect of receiving a distant Reiki treatment, if the energy flows, then they are on a subconscious level giving the required permission. If it doesn't flow to them, then they simply don't need it. Reiki is of a much higher vibration than the conscious minds of either the practitioner or the recipient. It is the manifestation of divine intelligence within the physical realm and we should not try to substitute our limited intelligence for it. When we practice our loving kindness meditation we don't ask for permission then, so why should there be a need to ask for permission before sending Reiki (the energy of love and compassion)? It is best to just let Reiki do its work in the way that it knows best.

The question of how a distant treatment works often comes up. Essentially, when we invoke the symbols, and Symbol 3, the Distant symbol is our primary tool in this we are using the power of our mind to send the qualities of those symbols to the individual that we wish to work on or with. This is possible due to our interconnectedness with all beings through our commonality as emanations of the Universal Energy Field. Through the use of the Reiki symbols, we connect to particular qualities and aspects of the Universal Energy Field, thus raising our own vibration to become an effective channel for the energy, and through the invocation of the qualities associated with the Distant symbol, are able to transfer this energy over any distance to another. Since we are all Mind, and time and space are constructs of this Mind, then it is possible for Mind to transcend its own creation. To really get to grips with how this is possible in any meaningful way, if not on an intellectual level but on an intuitive level, it is necessary to fully explore the nature of the Reiki symbols, particularly the Distant symbol. So again, if you have put these down, it might be worthwhile picking them up again and exploring them further.

## The Source of the Body's Disharmony

It is worth reflecting to a degree on the nature of the problems that we work with in using Reiki in a therapeutic setting. In developing our knowledge in this area, we are much more easily able to provide appropriate care and help for those in need, and ultimately as an expression of this understanding to invoke the requisite compassion that is so essential in a healing context.

All physical and psychological problems are the direct result of some degree of disharmony within the makeup of the individual. Each and every experience, illness and psychological problem that we may have or go through is there to teach us something. They are all tools for growth. Traumatic events and situations in our lives as well as minor hiccups that disturb our sense of peace have the effect of causing the brain to send chemical messages to particular cells within the body, which over time accumulate. The locations of these depend on the nature of the trauma. When we burn our finger on a match as a child we quickly, through the pain that is felt, learn not to play with matches. When we make the choice in life not to take heed of the lesson being offered, or decide to put it off until some later date, we start to gather stresses within the body that can penetrate very deeply and we can end up burning ourselves again, sometimes, many times over. As these stresses build and intensify creating an accumulation of negative debris within us, the more our lives and bodies will go out of balance. The body remembers everything. There is no point in blaming anyone else, or the circumstances of one's life. Firstly this is a denial of our own actions and reactions that have manifested these problems, but also because in doing so, we are denying our own responsibility in learning from them and we are not empowering ourselves to let them go. Whether or not we achieve a complete healing of our problems is not really the point, however. We try to achieve a quality of life that is empowering rather than dependent. As my Reiki Masters, Gordon and Dorothy Bell have noted, it is this quality of life that is important, not the absence of symptoms. So when we bring Reiki to bear on these problems we give the recipient choice. Sometimes the choice is not clear-cut. There is not always an opportunity to let the problem go and effect a complete healing. Sometimes the lesson to be learnt is to live with the problem, in the best way that we can and so increase the quality of life through the way that we orientate our minds to that which afflicts us. When there is a possibility of letting the problem go it is important that we learn whatever is to be learnt and change that aspect of ourselves that caused the problem in the first place. As Debbie Shapiro noted in her classic book *The Bodymind Workbook:*

> Understanding the bodymind language opens the door for
> us…to begin acknowledging, accepting and loving who we are,
> as we are, complete with whatever we find buried within us.
> In accepting what we find, we can begin the healing process. A
> healing relationship develops as we recognize the role we are
> playing in our own state of wellness, recognize what we need to

do in order to become free of limitations, and as we integrate the changes that take place as a result of that recognition; in other words, as we bring awareness and love to all aspects of our being.

So in bringing Reiki to bear on the problems that we all suffer, we expose them to an intense and very penetrating ray of love and compassion. In doing so, we start to uncover the roots of our illnesses or states of mental imbalance, often quite profoundly bringing them into direct conscious awareness. Where perhaps we had felt guilt or fear or worry or anxiety that had over time created toxic emotional residues in the body, we can now start to break down these destructive elements. Love (Reiki) and fear or worry or any other negative state cannot co-exist. We cannot feel fear and love at the same time. Again as Debbie Shapiro made clear:

> The future grows out of our present thoughts and attitudes, and we have the power to change those thoughts, however deeply ingrained they may be, at any time. Our understanding of life, our approach to it and our attitude towards ourselves and others, determines, to a very large extent, our state of ease or disease.

The way that we regard ourselves is the primary factor in our state of health. It is the place that we all need to start with to heal. If we cannot resolve issues that we may have about our own sense of self, then we don't stand much chance of correcting our thoughts in relation to others and the wider world. As the renowned Bernie Segal, amongst many others, has said, "…an unreserved, positive self-adoration remains the essence of health…" Learning to love ourselves is the first great step in restoring health, as the lack of self love was probably the first great step in destroying it, and this in some ways returns us to the essence of RJKD philosophy and practice — to heal the self on all levels to optimize our beneficial engagement with the world outside of ourselves.

## Picking Up Other People's Stuff

There is a lot said about this issue in many healing circles. Some people are scared off from engaging in healing work because they don't want to be 'contaminated' by other people's problems, illnesses, pains or 'stuff' in general. They feel that when they put their hands on, they might for instance feel a knotting in their stomach or a cramp in their leg and then discover that the recipient of the healing energy under their hands also suffers from this. They become worried that they are going to be left with the same pains or problems as the recipient once the treatment is over. This sort of response is based in fear and not compassion, and so will create a barrier between the recipient and the Reiki channel. We need to overcome this fear, which is simply our own resistance to experiencing 'the light', and merge with the Universal Energy Field and the person that we are working with.

Ric A Weinman had this to say in his book *How to Channel Healing Energy*:

> Many people misguidedly believe that if they are not careful when they release negative charges from someone they are working with, they will pick up this Stuff and absorb it into themselves. Many of these people also fear that they may pick up someone else's headache, exhaustion or even disease. They feel vulnerable because of the openness of the state they are in when they are channeling, and hence they have come up with methods for 'protecting' themselves.
>
> As common as these beliefs are, they have no validity whatsoever...
>
> What happens when you watch a person release sadness during a healing session is not very different from watching a film character go through some sad experience. And the deeper, more powerful the emotion the receiver is releasing, the deeper you may be triggered too. It is important to remember that whatever you are experiencing emotionally is

just your own emotional response – you are not picking up anything from the other person. Although a certain person may always trigger a particular feeling or resistance in you that makes it hard for you to stay clear (of 'negative' feelings), this unclarity is your own Stuff triggered but not caused by the other person…You are responsible for your own state of beingness, the only stuff you can ever have is your own.

Of course, if we have a strong enough fear of taking on someone else's problems, then as energy follows thought, there is a good possibility that we may create these same conditions for ourselves and indeed begin to suffer with the same symptoms as our client or recipient. We create the thing that we fear, but again, this is not being picked up from the other person, it is our own stuff that we manufacture through the creative power of fear and resistance.

At other times people feel that when they pick things up during a healing session, what they are doing is identifying or 'diagnosing' the problem or problem area in the recipient, and they see this as an entirely helpful situation, enabling them to direct the energy to specific regions of the body or to solve specific problems. We must remember in this however, that it is not wise at all to try to manipulate the Reiki energy to bring about specific desired outcomes. Reiki will do what is needed for the highest good of the recipient and this may not be what the recipient or the person channeling the energy feels is for the best. We can direct the energy to a degree, but it will ultimately go to wherever it is most needed in any case. We cannot choose to solve specific problems, only the Reiki energy in conjunction with the higher self (an aspect of Reiki) can do this.

It is then possible to pick up sensations of what the recipient of the energy is feeling. This is not a process of 'taking on' an illness and making it your own, it is more of an empathic tuning in to the rhythms of the recipient, and having a deep sense of the pain that they are going through. It is not really appropriate to call this a diagnostic procedure, and in some countries, like the UK, to engage with this sort of empathic response and to use it as a diagnostic procedure is in fact illegal. What we can say however is that this close identification with another's pain does provide us with an opportunity to develop our own compassion for their suffering and this in turn allows us to become much more effective as channels for healing energy. What we must try to avoid is the raising into consciousness of a negative reaction to whatever surfaces during the healing session. If we are mindful of our own mental process and the thoughts that arise as they arise, we can simply accept the feeling and let it go by staying detached. It is really all about having the proper mind set during the healing session.

## Using Intuition in a Healing Context

The development of intuitive abilities, along with the development and strengthening of other psychic abilities such as clairvoyance that can come about through the continual application of Reiki and meditation in our lives are valuable tools on our own spiritual journey and for guidance and inspiration as we make our way through life. The 2nd Degree attunements in particular can stimulate the development of our intuitive center located at the pituitary gland. To the Hindus it is known as *The Eye of Shiva*, in the West we generally refer to it as *The Third Eye*. As a consequence of the 2nd Degree attunements, the normal spherical waves of thought that emanate from this center are sharpened and focused to a much higher degree and do not dissipate as easily as they did prior to the attunements. It is also the case then that as a consequence of this heightened sensitivity that the mental vibrations from others are also received at this point much more easily. It is not uncommon however to find that these abilities can come to the fore and be accentuated whilst engaged in the process of giving someone a Reiki treatment, particularly if we are using this process to deepen our meditation practice with the *Six Point Meditation*. Often insights into the problems and life experiences of the person under our hands can reveal themselves. It is at this point that we must exercise a great deal of self-control and analysis, as well as professionalism in our dealing with this information. How do we know that what we perceive relates to the person that we are working on, and not to ourselves? The energy may be highlighting something within us. It is also very important to recognize that the picking up of psychic messages or information during a healing session is not a part of the healing process. In terms of the specific healing needs of the recipient, this information is not relevant. Clairvoyance, clairaudience, telepathy and all other forms of psychic ability are not a part of Reiki. Reiki heals without the need for this type of extraneous input. It is therefore advisable, especially if these types of ability are developing for the first time, to keep quiet about the received impressions. Because these types of psychic contact are filtered through the human mind and are therefore subject to various influences such as random thoughts, the voice of the mass consciousness and the interference of the ego, there is a good chance that what you believe to be a psychic impression is to some degree or another not entirely accurate. We need to differentiate between these influences and the voice of our Higher Selves. When being guided by the Higher Self there should be a sense of inner peace and harmony and a deep knowing that you are being guided correctly. If you listen to the intellect or the thoughts that arise as a consequence of its connection to the mass consciousness there is often an unsettled feeling. With practice it should be easy to discriminate between the two. The more you tune in to your intuition, the more it will develop. It is important however to reserve these abilities for your own use where through constant assessment and examination you can become familiar with how much you can personally trust your own instincts to be accurate. In this context they are a valuable tool, and enable us to take heed much more consciously of the guidance offered to us by our Higher Selves. This will allow us to live a life that is much more balanced and peaceful. We must learn however not to become too attached to these abilities as they are not the ultimate goal, but merely staging posts on the way.

## The View from Science

Fortunately as modern technology develops we are more and more easily able to measure the healing effects of emitted energy such as Reiki. Paula Horan noted in her book *The Ultimate Reiki Touch* that energy therapies such as Reiki are much more in line with the latest developments in quantum physics whilst modern Western medical theory and technique is still stuck in the Newtonian and Cartesian notions of separation and mechanistic intervention, which as time passes is being seen more and more as a rather bizarre aberration in the long history of healing methods. Many studies have been undertaken over the years to try to measure and quantify that which the scientific community at large generally regards as hokum. Fortunately there have been a few pioneers and open-minded individuals willing to put the claims made for energy healing to the test, and the results seem remarkable. As the author Daniel Reid has noted in talking about the curative properties of *Qi Gong*:

> Scientific studies demonstrating the curative power of chi-gung in almost every type of cancer have been presented at international medical conferences throughout the world… their results indicate that drugs, surgery, chemotherapy, radiation and other forms of expensive high-tech therapy favored by conventional modern medicine are not only less efficient…but actually further aggravate these conditions… sufficient numbers of professional Western physicians have now personally witnessed the curative powers of emitted chi under scientifically controlled conditions to bring medical chi-gung into serious scientific consideration in Western medical circles.

Some of the most astounding evidence for the efficacy of energy healing therapies has come from the psychologist William Braud at the 'Mind Science Foundation' of San Antonio, Texas. Over a period of 17 years and using only untrained volunteers that had no prior experience of engaging in any form of healing therapy, Braud attempted to show that it was possible to influence the nervous system of a group of participants, mentally from a distance.

One group, known as 'receivers' were wired up to machines that measured seven physiological responses, such as blood pressure, muscle tremor and skin conductivity. The second group, known as 'senders' were asked to either calm or arouse the receivers simply by thinking about them. The 'senders' were located in a room some distance from the 'receivers'. In total Braud conducted 37 experiments that involved 449 volunteers working across 665 individual sessions. Braud discovered that at the exact moment that the sender was asked to begin thinking about the receiver, there was a measurable change in the receiver's physiological condition. At the conclusion of all of the experiments, the results were shocking in their total vindication of that which healers and others have been claiming for many centuries. The odds in favour of distant mental interactions between people were a staggering 100 trillion to one against chance. Not even widely available commercial drugs can make such a claim. Aspirin, for instance, as an aid in preventing heart attacks did not show anywhere near the level of success when first tested for release on to the market as a heart attack preventative, as the tests for distant healing in Braud's studies. If this is the sort of result that can be obtained from a group of untrained volunteers, then what of studies on those who have been trained to channel healing energy?

Of the many other studies conducted into the mind's ability to influence and heal over a distance, one of the most widely known is that of Dr Robert Becker and Dr John Zimmerman of the University of Colorado. In the 1980s and with the use of a Superconducting Quantum Interference Device (SQUID) they tried to establish exactly what happens when people practice therapies such as Reiki. What they found was that the brain wave patterns of the receiver and practitioner became synchronized in the alpha state, characteristic of deep relaxation and meditation. It was interesting to note that the brain waves also pulsed in unison with the Earth's biomagnetic field, known as the Schuman Resonance. At these times the biomagnetic field surrounding the hands of the practitioners was at least 1000 times greater than normal, and not a result of the body's internal current. When the same experiments were conducted on 'sham' healers, no such changes in the energy field occurred. Toni Bunnel has put forward the idea that the link between the energy field of the earth and that of the practitioner enables the practitioner to draw from the Universal Energy Field via the Schuman Resonance.

There are many theories being postulated on the actual mechanism that makes distant healing in particular possible. One of the theories that is currently being discussed is described by Richard Gordon in his book *Quantum Touch:*

> ...when two systems are oscillating at different frequencies, there is an impelling force called resonance that causes the two to transfer energy from one to another. When two similarly tuned systems vibrate at different frequencies there is another aspect of this energy transfer called entrainment, which causes them to line up and to vibrate at the same frequency. Entrainment is the process by which things align their movement and energy together to match in rhythm and phase.

This happens for instance when two clocks, with pendulums swinging out of phase and at different rates, are hung together on a wall. Through the medium of the wall, over time they will transfer energy so that eventually, the pendulums will perfectly synchronize. This process of entrainment as a theory for the explanation of distant energetic interactions is very much supported by the research work into the process of distant healing by Becker and Zimmerman when they noted the entraining of the brain wave patterns. The two systems, through the conscious intent of one – the practitioner – match and then synchronize. So in essence this brings us back to where we started and the need as expressed so fundamentally and urgently within the RJKD system, to work extensively upon ourselves as a priority. If we do not do so, then when we engage in a healing process, we induce the state of synchronicity with the receiver, but as our own vibratory rate is not actually that high, then our efforts are relatively limited in their effects. As we raise our own vibration, closer and closer to that of the Universal Energy Field through constant self-practice, then when entrainment occurs with a Reiki recipient, it happens at a much higher level through the process of raising their vibration up to meet our own. In this way we open the door to the infinite.

# 12
# Out of the Shadows

The cave you fear to enter holds the treasure you seek.
*Joseph Campbell*

Following a number of years in which the teachings of Reiki Jin Kei Do were being quietly disseminated around the globe, the decision was taken by Ranga in 2005, 15 years after Seiji's transmission of the system, to initiate a sweeping review of where the lineage stands in relation to the wider world of Reiki and to its own core values. It was decided that the time was right to substantially raise the profile of the lineage and teachings and set up an international Training Center for those already trained in the RJKD system and as a central resource for those interested in this unique system of spiritual development and Reiki practice. To this end, during 2005, many Masters and students of the lineage were engaged in a substantive review and discussion process via a private Internet Forum. The resultant Center is planned to be the hub of a global network of nationally and regionally based Training Centers and a common reference point for all those teaching RJKD and *Buddho-EnerSense*.

The lineage has moved on and changed a great deal over the last few years and divergence of approach has naturally taken place as teachers have gone their own way with the material that they were initially given. It has now become very clear that there is a need to enforce core standards within the lineage so that RJKD, as a coherent and specific branch of the Reiki family, will develop a much more consistent approach to the transmission of its teachings and will have moved further down the road to defining more precisely its fundamental values and thus its own identity. The role of Lineage Representatives in various parts of the globe is therefore being substantially reviewed and may be devolved to groups of Masters within specified regions or countries to ensure that standards in practice are maintained within their locality and to oversee the official certification of new Reiki Masters upon their meeting of the established criteria for teaching.

One other outcome of this wide-ranging review process is the production by Ranga of a set of manuals to preserve in an unadulterated form the teachings that were transmitted to him by Seiji. These are not designed to be a RJKD Masters sole teaching materials, but a reference work for the Master and students to draw upon. Each Master has a unique approach to the delivery of the system and this is an important aspect of any teaching process. The manuals serve as a point of common understanding of the Core Teachings of RJKD and thus provide a benchmark for the Lineage Representatives and individual Masters to work to.

It has long been an ambition of Ranga's to set up such an international Center, which will ultimately operate not only as the global focus for the RJKD lineage, but also as a multi-therapy healing center in its own right, where clients can receive intensive treatment from a number of practitioners skilled in a variety of therapeutic disciplines. The focus of the Center shall remain predominantly orientated to the practice of Reiki and meditation however, and it is expected, once the Center is fully functioning, that a number of RJKD practitioners will be able to work there. The name given to the new organization is ***The International***

### *Reiki Jin Kei Do and Buddho-EnerSense Training Centre*.

The Center is becoming a primary focus for RJKD Masters and students worldwide for further training, to run their own RJKD or *Buddho-EnerSense*-orientated seminars and to contribute to the establishment of an extensive scientific research programme into the effects of energy healing disciplines, most specifically, Reiki. The global network of Centers have a role in supporting all of this work through their own engagement with the healing disciplines of meditation and Reiki therapeutics as well as the ongoing dissemination of the RJKD and *Buddho-EnerSense* teachings.

The Center website is designed to provide general information on the teachings of RJKD and *Buddho-EnerSense* (address given in the following Directory) and as a common reference point for individual Master and practitioner members of the lineage to keep abreast of new developments. A new Forum has been established for the website to allow RJKD practitioners and Masters to communicate with each other, share experiences, and importantly to maintain contact with the lineage head. In time, this may also include video conferencing and other interactive facilities.

This is an exciting time for Reiki Jin Kei Do, and hopefully for the wider Reiki community. Whilst honoring the excellent work of all of those seriously engaged with Reiki in whatever setting and from whichever lineage, it has always been known within RJKD that this lineage does indeed hold elements of practice and historical information that has either not been transmitted down other lines of teachers, or has yet not been made public by those who might hold the same material. With the emergence of Reiki Jin Kei Do as a major player in the world of Reiki it is very much hoped that what Reiki Jin Kei Do can offer may enrich the wider Reiki community's collective experience of this wonderful healing and personal development practice for the betterment of all of us and ultimately of all of mankind. As a discreet and coherent approach to Reiki however, RJKD aims to hold to its central philosophic orientation to its practice and teachings and not become encumbered by the addition of Reiki methods imported from other lineages or traditions. What we have is what we need, but individual teachers may develop points of practice in their own way by the addition of supportive methods that enhance the Core Teachings as they see fit. What needs to be avoided is a process of ossification. The lineage is very much an evolving system of thought and practice and as with everything else, as time goes by, further change and evolution will be inevitable.

# Directory of Masters

All of the following Reiki Masters are currently offering training in the lineage of Reiki Jin Kei Do. If you are interested in taking a class, they would be more than happy to hear from you. Many Masters listed by State for Australia, South Africa and the US also teach in other parts of their respective countries, so it is always worth contacting some to see if they can arrange a class nearer to you if there is no one local.

This is not an exhaustive list as it was not possible to contact everyone prior to the completion of this book, so if you are looking for training in a country not listed, please either go to the Reiki Jin Kei Do website given below or contact the author at: *SGooch@omahhum.org*

Any RJKD Masters not included here that would like their details in future editions of the book are invited to send their details to the author.

**The International Reiki Jin Kei Do and Buddho-Ener-Sense Training Centre** can be found at: *www.reikijinkeido.net*

## Argentina

Silvia Ariki
 *E-mail:* silviaariki@yahoo.co.au
 *Website:* www.silviaariki.com

## Australia

### New South Wales

Dr Ranga J Premaratna PhD (*Lineage Head*)
 *Tel:* +61 2 9969 3920
 *E-mail:* ranga@reikijinkeido.net
 *Website:* www.reikijinkeido.net

Felix Yap
 *Tel:* +61 2 0414 538 995
 *E-mail:* felix_yap@dlcsoft.com.au
 *Website:* reiki.dlcsoft.com.au

Bruce Lonsdale
 *Tel:* +61 269 273 395
 *E-mail:* bllonsdale@yahoo.com

Paul Daniel
 *Tel:* +61 412 302 896
 *E-mail:* pdaniel1828@yahoo.com.au

Jeanette Sharpe
 *Tel:* +61 2 9969 1487
 *E-mail:* jeannettesharpe@hotmail.com

Louise Holcombe
 *Tel:* +61 2 6921 7654
 *E-mail:* lholcombe@bigpond.net.au

### Queensland

Ann Smith
 *Tel:* +61 7 3315 6088

Evania
 *E-mail:* evania77@hotmail.com

Faye Wenke
  *Tel:* +61 4 1277 8205
  *E-mail:* faye@reiki-lifeunlimited.com
  *Website:* www.reiki-lifeunlimited.com

Glenys Randall
  *Tel:* +61 7 3806 5671
  *E-mail:* glenysr@optusnet.com.au

Helena Ryan-Scully
  *Tel:* +61 4 1450 5620
  *E-mail:* helena10@bigpond.net.au

Kaylene Hay
  *Tel:* +61 7 0428 8474 66
  *E-mail:* kaylenehay@yahoo.com

Lynette Creber
  *Tel:* +61 7 4954 0580
  *E-mail:* lynncreber@bigpond.com

Roz Bishop
  *Tel:* +61 7 4036 2003
  *E-mail:* rozbishop@iig.com.au

Sherise Kaye
  *Tel:* +61 7 5448 3013

Leonie Bartlett
  *Tel:* +61 7 5456 1849
  *E-mail:* leonieb16@bigpond.com.au

Kathleen Smyth
  *Tel:* +61 7 4946 1110
  *E-mail:* kfsmyth@bigpond.com

### *Victoria*

Eileen Chapman
  *Tel:* +61 3 9482 5336
  *E-mail:* eilchap@yahoo.com
  *Website:* www.geocities.com/uskreiki

Jim Frew
 *Tel:* +61 3 5983 9971
 *E-mail:* Jim.Frew@r150.aone.net.au
 *Website:* www.geocities.com/jkdreiki

## Bahamas/Bermuda/Caribbean Islands

Steve Gooch
 *Tel:* +44 1788 579550
 *E-mail:* SGooch@omahhum.org
 *Website:* www.omahhum.org

## Bahrain

Munira Al-Fadhel
 *Tel:* +973 3969 7856
 *E-mail:* alfadelm@batelco.com.bh

## Belgium

Tony Birdfield
 *Tel:* +44 1202 601412
 *E-mail:* tbirdfield@aol.com

## Canada

Patricia Warren
 *Tel:* +1 508 528 5888
 *E-mail:* pkw2@mindspring.com
 *Website:* www.rekijinkeido.com

## Denmark

Gordon and Dorothy Bell
 *Tel:* +44 1225 852404
 *E-mail:* GandDBell@aol.com
 *Website:* www.healing-touch.co.uk

# Egypt

Steve Gooch
*Tel:* +44 1788 579550
*E-mail:* SGooch@omahhum.org
*Website:* www.omahhum.org

## Eire

Tony Birdfield
*Tel:* +44 1202 601412
*E-mail:* tbirdfield@aol.com

## France

Fiona Robertson
*Tel:* +33 559 54 5635
*E-mail:* fionaroma@yahoo.co.uk

Terence Coleman and Edith Izsak-Coleman
*Tel:* +33 3 8697 6237
*E-mail:* nid.du.geai@wanadoo.fr
*Website:* www.nid-du-geai.com

Steve Gooch
*Tel:* +44 1788 579550
*E-mail:* SGooch@omahhum.org
*Website:* www.omahhum.org

Gordon and Dorothy Bell
*Tel:* +44 1225 852404
*E-mail:* GandDBell@aol.com
*Website:* www.healing-touch.co.uk

Tony Birdfield
*Tel:* +44 1202 601412
*E-mail:* tbirdfield@aol.com

## Germany

Gordon and Dorothy Bell
*Tel:* +44 1225 852404
*E-mail:* GandDBell@aol.com
*Website:* www.healing-touch.co.uk

David Price
*Tel:* +44 771 727 8345
*E-mail:* DavidPrice@channel-reiki.com
*Website:* www.channel-reiki.com

Tony Birdfield
*Tel:* +44 1202 601412
*E-mail:* tbirdfield@aol.com

## Greece

Steve Gooch
*Tel:* +44 1788 579550
*E-mail:* SGooch@omahhum.org
*Website:* www.omahhum.org

## Holland

Anita Zih-De Haan
*Tel:* +31 1041 54250
*E-mail:* anita.zih@planet.nl

David Price
*Tel:* +44 771 727 8345
*E-mail:* DavidPrice@channel-reiki.com
*Website:* www.channel-reiki.com

Tony Birdfield
*Tel:* +44 1202 601412
*E-mail:* tbirdfield@aol.com

## Iceland

Gordon and Dorothy Bell
  *Tel:* +44 1225 852404
  *E-mail:* GandDBell@aol.com
  *Website:* www.healing-touch.co.uk

## India

Steve Gooch
  *Tel:* +44 1788 579550
  *E-mail:* SGooch@omahhum.org
  *Website:* www.omahhum.org

## Italy

Steve Gooch
  *Tel:* +44 1788 579550
  *E-mail:* SGooch@omahhum.org
  *Website:* www.omahhum.org

Silvia Ariki
  *E-mail:* silviaariki@yahoo.com.au
  *Website:* www.silviaariki.com

## Japan

Gordon and Dorothy Bell
  *Tel:* +44 1225 852404
  *E-mail:* GandDBell@aol.com
  *Website:* www.healing-touch.co.uk

## Kuwait

Munira Al-Fadhel
  *Tel:* +973 3969 7856
  *E-mail:* alfadelm@batelco.bh

## Lebanon

Patricia Warren
*Tel:* +1 508 528 5888
*E-mail:* pkw2@mindspring.com
*Website:* www.reikijinkeido.com

## Lithuania/Latvia

Patricia Warren
*Tel:* +1 508 528 5888
*E-mail:* pkw2@mindspring.com
*Website:* www.reikijinkeido.com

## Malta

Steve Gooch
*Tel:* +44 1788 579550
*E-mail:* SGooch@omahhum.org
*Website:* www.omahhum.org

## Nepal

Kunzang Dechen Chodron
*Tel:* +1 319 624 7095
*E-mail:* kunzang@reikishindo.org
*Website:* www.reikishindo.org

## New Zealand

Lynette Creber
*Tel:* +61 7 4954 0580
*E-mail:* lynncreber@bigpond.com

## Oman

Munira Al-Fadhel
*Tel:* +973 3969 7856
*E-mail:* alfadelm@batelco.com.bh

## Poland

Patricia Warren
  *Tel:* +1 508 528 5888
  *E-mail:* pkw2@mindspring.com
  *Website:* www.reikijinkeido.com

## Puerto Rico

Patricia Warren
  *Tel:* +1 508 528 5888
  *E-mail:* pkw2@mindspring.com
  *Website:* www.reikijinkeido.com

## Qatar

Munira Al-Fadhel
  *Tel:* +973 3969 7856
  *E-mail:* alfadelm@batelco.com.bh

## Russia

Andrei Kovalenko
  *E-mail:* webmaster@shambala.ru
  *Website:* www.shambala.ru/reiki/

Sedova Dinara
  *Tel:* +70 95 687 5210
  *E-mail:* cheta@online.ru

Patricia Warren
  *Tel:* +1 508 528 5888
  *E-mail:* pkw2@mindspring.com
  *Website:* www.reikijinkeido.com

## Saudi Arabia

Munira Al-Fadhel
  *Tel:* +973 3969 7856
  *E-mail:* alfadelm@batelco.com.bh

## South Africa

### Gauteng

Anne De Lima
  *Tel:* +27 11 896 3772
  *E-mail:* annedelima@telkomsa.net

Jenny van der Merwe
  *Tel:* +27 11 913 3155
  *E-mail:* ladyrainbow@telkomsa.net
  *Website:* www.energycolors.com

Elsabe Booyens
  *Tel:* +27 82 905 6946
  *E-mail:* elsabeb@hotmail.com

Marleen de Villiers
  *Tel:* +27 82 898 1159
  *E-mail:* violet@iafrica.com

### Kwa-Zulunatal

Michelle Botha
  *Tel:* +27 83 660 8281

### Mpumalanga

Sharlie Opperman
  *Tel:* +27 13 697 4102
  *E-mail:* oppermanhc@tut.ac.za

### Western Cape

Ann Gadd
  *Tel:* +27 21 554 1235
  *E-mail:* anngadd@netconnect.co.za
  *Website:* www.anngadd.co.za

Valentine Lange
  *Tel:* +27 23 541 1872
  *E-mail:* bijlia@intekom.co.za
  *Website:* www.karooretreat.com

Sacha Want
  *Tel:* +27 22 492 3660
  *E-mail:* sashc@iafrica.com

## Spain

Silvia Ariki
  *E-mail:* silviaariki@yahoo.com.au
  *Website:* www.silviaariki.com

Dennis Austen
  *Tel:* +34 96 295 0230
  *E-mail:* dennisausten@hotmail.com

Steve Gooch
  *Tel:* +44 1788 579550
  *E-mail:* SGooch@omahhum.org
  *Website:* www.omahhum.org

Gordon and Dorothy Bell
  *Tel:* +44 1225 852404
  *E-mail:* GandDBell@aol.com
  *Web-site:* www.healing-touch.co.uk

Tony Birdfield
  *Tel:* +44 1202 601412
  *E-mail:* tbirdfield@aol.com

Patricia Warren
  *Tel:* +1 508 528 5888
  *E-mail:* pkw2@mindspring.com
  *Website:* www.reikijinkeido.com

## Tanzania

Steve Gooch
  *Tel:* +44 1788 579550
  *E-mail:* SGooch@omahhum.org
  *Website:* www.omahhum.org

## Ukraine

Patricia Warren
   *Tel:* +1 508 528 5888
   *E-mail:* pkw2@mindspring.com
   *Website:* www.rekijinkeido.com

## United Arab Emirates

   Munira Al-Fadhel
   *Tel:* +973 3969 7856
   *E-mail:* alfadelm@batelco.com.bh

## United Kingdom

Gordon and Dorothy Bell
   *Tel:* +44 1225 852404
   *E-mail:* GandDBell@aol.com
   *Website:* www.healing-touch.co.uk

Steve Gooch
   *Tel:* +44 1788 579550
   *E-mail:* SGooch@omahhum.org
   *Website:* www.omahhum.org

Judith Cabral
   *Tel:* +44 1676 534 815
   *E-mail:* judy.cabral@tiscali.co.uk

David Price
   *Tel:* +44 771 727 8345
   *E-mail:* DavidPrice@channel-reiki.com
   *Website:* www.channel-reiki.com

Eric Anderson
   *Tel:* +44 1505 502678

Pam Ballard
   *Tel:* +44 1942 239735

Tony Birdfield
   *Tel:* +44 1202 601412
   *E-mail:* tbirdfield@aol.com

Karin Elder
  *Tel:* +44 7801 733222
  *E-mail:* karin@whatcrofthall.freeserve.co.uk

Sarah Owen
  *Tel:* +44 1206 366819
  *E-mail:* sarahowen1@hotmail.com

Faye Wenke
  *Tel:* +61 412 778 205
  *E-mail:* faye@reiki-lifeunlimited.com
  *Website:* www.reiki-lifeunlimited.com

Patricia Warren
  *Tel:* +1 508 528 5888
  *E-mail:* pkw2@mindspring.com
  *Website:* www.reikijinkeido.com

## US

### *Arkansas*

Ellis Widner
  *Tel:* +1 501 666 7395
  *E-mail:* pemadorje@mac.com

### *California*

Rev. Julie Shepard
  *Tel:* +1 510 502 9192
  *E-mail:* paradiseministries_els@yahoo.com
  *Website:* www.paradiseministries.info

Salina Rain
  *Tel:* +1 707 668 5408
  *E-mail:* astro@salinarain.com
  *Website:* www.salinarain.com

### *Florida*

Steve Gooch
  *Tel:* +44 1788 579550

*E-mail:* SGooch@omahhum.org
*Website:* www.omahhum.org

## *Iowa*

Cathy Bernsten
  *Tel:* +1 319 338 2826
  *E-mail:* reikimomu@hotmail.com
  *Website:* www.reikishindo.org

Denny Kelly
  *Tel:* +1 515 321 8987
  *E-mail:* DennyWKelly@hotmail.com

Kunzang Dechen Chodron
  *Tel:* +1 319 624 7095
  *E-mail:* kunzang@reikishindo.org
  *Website:* www.reikishindo.org

Michael Santangelo and Candida Maurer
  *Tel:* +1 319 351 3262
  *E-mail:* eastwindschool@yahoo.com
  *Website:* www.eastwindschool.com

Jennifer Wolffe
  *Tel:* +1 319 621 3717
  *E-mail:* j.wolffe@mchsi.com

## *Massachusetts*

Christine Radice
  *Tel:* +1 617 782 1681
  *E-mail:* christineradice@yahoo.com
  *Website:* www.bostonreiki.com

Laurie Wallace
  *Tel:* +1 781 784 2842
  *E-mail:* LaurieLWallace@msn.com

Nancy Silva
  *Tel:* +1 781 266 7228
  *E-mail:* nancy@reikirising.com
  *Website:* www.reikirising.com

Patricia Warren
  *Tel:* +1 508 528 5888
  *E-mail:* pkw2@mindspring.com
  *Website:* www.reikijinkeido.com

Susie Rosenwasser
  *Tel:* +1 781 784 7135
  *E-mail:* srosewater@comcast.net

## New Jersey

Bill Stevens
  *Tel:* +1 732 895 2154
  *E-mail:* wastevens@aol.com
  *Website:* www.billsreiki.com

## Oregon

Faye Wenke
  *Tel:* +61 412 778 205
  *E-mail:* faye@reiki-lifeunlimited.com
  *Website:* www.reiki-lifeunlimited.com

## Rhode Island

Katherine Harrop
  *Tel:* +1 401 846 5605
  *E-mail:* katherine@reiki-jin-kei-do.com
  *Website:* www.reiki-ji-kei-do.com

## Vermont

Dechen Drolkar and Mari Cordes
  *Tel:* +1 802 453 7318
  *E-mail:* dechen@direcway.com
  *Website:* www.homepage.mac.com/dechend

## Virginia

Karla Moffet
  *Tel:* +1 703 818 1789
  *E-mail:* omegatheend@msn.com

Gail Condrick
  *Tel:* +1 703 802 1111
  *E-mail:* gaileskew@cox.net
  *Website:* www.niavisions.com

Juanita Acevedo
  *Tel:* +1 703 273 5127
  *E-mail:* juanitaacevedo@msn.com
  *Web-site:* www.RaysofHealing.org

Linda Graziano Gasson
  *Tel:* +1 703 930 9333
  *E-mail:* linda@somaleadership.com
  *Website:* www.somaleadership.com

Nadine Wormsbacher
  *Tel:* +1 703 971 0065
  *E-mail:* nw57@cornell.edu

Stella Koch
  *Tel:* +1 703 759 5453
  *E-mail:* smkoch@aol.com
  *Website:* www.stellakoch.com

Gilbert Gallego
  *Tel:* +1 703 385 1019
  *E-mail:* gilbertgallego@comcast.net

### *Washington DC*

Gordon and Dorothy Bell
  *Tel:* +44 1225 852404
  *E-mail:* GandDBell@aol.com
  *Website:* www.healing-touch.co.uk

## US Virgin Islands

Patricia Warren
  *Tel:* +1 508 528 5888
  *E-mail:* pkw2@mindspring.com
  *Website:* www.reikijinkeido.com

## Yemen

Munira Al-Fadhel
  *Tel:* +973 3969 7856
  *E-mail:* alfadelm@batelco.com.bh

## Zimbabwe

Ruth Winkler
  *Tel:* +263 9 286739
  *E-mail:* ruth.winkler@gatorzw.com

# Bibliography

Arai, Yusei. *Shingon Esoteric Buddhism – A Handbook for Followers,* Shingon Buddhist International Institute, Fresno, 1997.

Barasch, Marc Ian. *Field Notes on the Compassionate Life,* Rodale Inc, Emmaus, 2005.

Bear, Kiana. *The History and Philosophy of Ayurveda and Ayurvedic Acupuncture,* ACAM Publishing, Australia, 1999.

Bell, Gordon. *Reiki Jin Kei Do,* in Reiki Magazin, 2001.

Bell, Gordon and Dorothy. *1st Degree Manual,* Unpublished, 1996.

Bell, Gordon and Dorothy. *2nd Degree Manual,* Unpublished, 1996.

Bell, Gordon and Dorothy. *3rd Degree Manual,* Unpublished, 1997.

Bhanti, Y Wimala. *Lessons of the Lotus – Practical Spiritual Teachings of a Traveling Buddhist Monk,* Piatkus, London, 1998.

Bhattachanya, Anupama. *A Touch of Death…or Life,* www.lifepositive. com, 2005.

Birdfield, Tony. *The Sacred Tree of Energy,* Unpublished MA dissertation, 2004.

Boeree, Dr C George. *The Basics of Buddhist Wisdom,* www.ship.edu. com, 2005.

Borang, Kajsa Krishni. *Principles of Reiki*, Thorsons, London, 1997.

Brecher, Paul. *Principles of Tai Chi,* Thorsons, London, 1997.

Charlish, Anne and Robertshaw, Angela. *Secrets of Reiki,* Dorling Kindersley, London, 2001.

Chuen, Master Lam Kam. *The Way of Energy*, Gaia Books, London, 1991.

Covey, Stephen R. *The 7 Habits of Highly Effective People*, Simon and Schuster, London, 1999.

Clifford, Terry. *The Diamond Healing*, Crucible, Wellingborough, 1989.

Cozort, Daniel. *Highest Yoga Tantra*, Snow Lion Publications, Ithaca, 1986.

Dhammika, Ven S. *Wisdom and Compassion – Good Questions, Good Answers*, www.buddhanet.net, 2005.

Doi, Hiroshi. *Modern Reiki Method for Healing*, Fraser Journal Publishing, British Columbia, 2000.

Draganescu, Mihai. *The Frontiers of Science and Self Organization*, www.racai.ro, 2005.

Eastcott, Michal J. *The Silent Path*, Rider, London, 1989.

Ellis, Richard. *Reiki and the Seven Chakras*, Vermilion, London, 2002.

Ellyard, Lawrence. *Reiki Healer – A Complete Guide to the Path and Practice of Reiki,* Lotus Press, Twin Lakes, 2004.

Emerson, Barbara. *Self-Healing Reiki,* Frog Ltd, Berkeley, 2001.

Flanagan, Anthony. *Buddhist Meditation – The Four Foundations of Mindfulness*, www.buddhism.about.com, 2005.

Gablik, Suzi. *A New Front,* in Resurgence Magazine, No 223, 2004.

Gach, Michael Reed. *Acupressure – How to Cure Common Ailments the Natural Way,* Piatkus, London, 1997.

Gooch, Steve. *Introduction to Meditation*, Unpublished article, 1999.

Gooch, Steve. *1st Degree Manual*, Unpublished, 2002.

Gooch, Steve. *2nd Degree Manual,* Unpublished, 2002.

Gooch, Steve. *3rd Degree Manual*, Unpublished, 2002.

Gordon, Richard. *Quantum Touch – The Power to Heal*, North Atlantic Books, Berkeley, 2002.

Harris, Elizabeth J. *Detachment and Compassion in Early Buddhism*, www.enabling.org, 1997.

Harrison, Eric. *How Meditation Heals*, Piatkus, London, 2000.

Hensel, Rev Thomas A and Emery, Rev Kevin Ross. *The Lost Steps of Reiki — The Channeled Teachings of Wei Chi*, Lightlines Publishing, Portsmouth, 1997.

Holm, Rolf. *Positive Thinking*, in Reiki Magazine International, Vol 6, No 2, 2004.

Horan, Paula. *Empowerment Through Reiki*, Lotus Light/Shangri-La, Twin Lakes, 1996.

Horan, Paula. *Reiki — 108 Questions and Answers*, Full Circle, Delhi, 1998.

Horan, Paula. *The Ultimate Reiki Touch,* Lotus Press/Shangri-La, Twin Lakes, 2002.

Jacka, Judy. *Health and Healing — With Special Reference to the Teachings of Alice Bailey*, World Goodwill, London, date unknown.

Janakabhivamsa, Chanmay Sayadavi Ashin. *Samatha and Vipassana Meditation*, Blue Mountains Insight Meditation Center, 1998.

Kelly, Maureen J. *Reiki and the Healing Buddha*, Lotus Press, Twin Lakes, 2000.

Khema, Aya. *When the Iron Eagle Flies — Buddhism for the West*, Arkana, London, 1991.

Khema, Aya. *Who Is Myself? A Guide to Buddhist Meditation*, Wisdom Publications, Boston, 1997.

Klinger-Omenka, Ursula. *Reiki with Gemstones*, Lotus Light/Shangri-La, Twin Lakes, 1997.

Kornfield, Jack. *A Path with Heart — A Guide Through the Perils and Promises of Spiritual Life*, Rider, London, 1994.

Kriger, Jeff. *Buddhist Compassion — Removing Suffering and Giving Joy*, www.sgi-usa.org, 2005.

Krishna, Gopi. *The Awakening of Kundalini*, Institute for Consciousness Research, Ontario, 1993.

Kushner, Harold S. *The Lord Is My Shepherd — Healing Wisdom of the Twenty-Third Psalm*, Anchor Books, New York, 2004.

Low, James. *Simply Being — Texts in the Dzogchen Tradition*, Vajra Press, London, 1994.

Lubeck, Walter. *Reiki — Way of the Heart*, Lotus Light/Shangri-La, Twin Lakes, 1996.

Lubeck, Walter et al. *The Spirit of Reiki*, Lotus Press, Twin Lakes, 2001.

McCoy, Dr Dorothy. *Trauma and Worry*, www.pioneerthinking.com, 2005.

McDaniel, Barbara. *Is Reiki Complementary Medicine?* in Reiki Magazine International, Vol 6, No 2, 2004.

Mitchell, Karyn. *Reiki – A Torch in Daylight*, Mind Rivers Publications, St Charles, 1994.

Parkes, Chris and Penny. *Reiki*, Vermilion, London, 1998.

Petter, Frank Arjava et al. *The Hayashi Reiki Manual*, Lotus Press/ Shangri-La, Twin Lakes, 2003.

Plamintr, Sunthorn. *Buddhist Meditation*, www.buddhismtoday.com, 2005.

Premaratna, Ranga. *1st Degree Manual*, Unpublished, 1998.

Premaratna, Ranga. *2nd Degree Manual*, Unpublished, 1998.

Premaratna, Ranga. *3rd Degree Manual*, Unpublished, 1998.

Premaratna, Ranga. *Reiki Jin Kei Do*, www.enersense.org, 1998.

Rand, William. *Reiki – The Healing Touch*, Vision Publications, 1995.

Rajsuddhinanamongkol, Phra. *Advantages of Chanting and How to Practice Vipassana Meditation,* Suchitra Ronruen, Bangok, 1997.

Reid, Daniel. *Chi Gung – Harnessing the Power of the Universe*, Simon and Schuster, London, 1998.

Reid, Howard. *The Book of Soft Martial Arts,* Gaia Books Limited, London, 1988.

Rinpoche, Ven Khandro. *Compassion and Wisdom,* www.shambhalasun. com, 2000.

Rinpoche, Sogyal. *The Tibetan Book of Living and Dying,* Rider, London, 1996.

Rinpoche, Tenzin Wangyal. *Healing with Form, Energy and Light*, Snow Lion Publications, Ithaca, 2002.

Rowland, Amy Z. *Traditional Reiki for Our Times,* Healing Arts Press, Rochester, 1998.

Saraswati, Swami Ambikananda. *Principles of Breathwork,* Thorsons, London, 1999.

Shapiro, Debbie. *The Bodymind Workbook,* Element Books, Shaftesbury, 1991.

Shuffrey, Sandi Leir. *Teach Yourself Reiki,* Hodder Headline Plc, London, 2000.

Siegel MD, Bernie S. *Love, Medicine and Miracles,* Harper Perennial, New York, 1990.

St. Ruth, Diana and Richard. *Simple Guide to Theravada Buddhism,* Global Books Ltd, Folkestone,1998.

Stein, Diane. *Essential Reiki,* The Crossing Press Inc, Freedom, 1996.

Stiene, Bronwen and Frans. *The Reiki Sourcebook,* O Books, Winchester, 2004.

Stiene, Bronwen and Frans. *The Japanese Art of Reiki,* O Books, Winchester, 2005.

Tharchin, Sermey Khensur Lobsang. *The Essence of Mahayana Lojong Practice,* Mahayana Sutra and Tantra Press, Howell, 1998.

Vennells, David F. *Reiki for Beginners,* Llewelyn Publications, St Paul, 1999.

Vennells, David F. *Reiki Mastery – For Second Degree Students and Masters,* O Books, Winchester, 2005.

Vessantara. *Meeting the Buddhas,* Windhorse Publications, Birmingham, 1998.

Wattles, Wallace D. *The Science of Getting Rich,* Certain Way Productions, Seattle, 2002.

Weinman, Ric A. *How to Channel Healing Energy,* Thorsons, London, 1997.

Young, Shinzen. *How Meditation Works,* www.shinzen.org, 2005.

Young, Shinzen. *Purpose and Method of Vipassana Meditation,* www.shinzen.org, 2005.

# Other Resources

www.threshold.ca/reiki
www.sivasakti.com
www.reiki-evolution.co.uk
www.healing-touch.co.uk
www.reiki.org
www.samurai-archives.com
www.usui-do.org

# O

is a symbol of the world,
of oneness and unity. O Books
explores the many paths of wholeness and spiritual understanding which
different traditions have developed down
the ages. It aims to bring this knowledge in
accessible form, to a general readership, providing practical spirituality to today's seekers.

**For the full list of over 200 titles covering:**
ACADEMIC/THEOLOGY • ANGELS • ASTROLOGY/
NUMEROLOGY • BIOGRAPHY/AUTOBIOGRAPHY
• BUDDHISM/ENLIGHTENMENT • BUSINESS/LEADERSHIP/
WISDOM • CELTIC/DRUID/PAGAN • CHANNELLING
• CHRISTIANITY; EARLY • CHRISTIANITY; TRADITIONAL
• CHRISTIANITY; PROGRESSIVE • CHRISTIANITY;
DEVOTIONAL • CHILDREN'S SPIRITUALITY • CHILDREN'S
BIBLE STORIES • CHILDREN'S BOARD/NOVELTY • CREATIVE
SPIRITUALITY • CURRENT AFFAIRS/RELIGIOUS • ECONOMY/
POLITICS/SUSTAINABILITY • ENVIRONMENT/EARTH
• FICTION • GODDESS/FEMININE • HEALTH/FITNESS
• HEALING/REIKI • HINDUISM/ADVAITA/VEDANTA
• HISTORY/ARCHAEOLOGY • HOLISTIC SPIRITUALITY
• INTERFAITH/ECUMENICAL • ISLAM/SUFISM
• JUDAISM/CHRISTIANITY • MEDITATION/PRAYER
• MYSTERY/PARANORMAL • MYSTICISM • MYTHS
• POETRY • RELATIONSHIPS/LOVE • RELIGION/
PHILOSOPHY • SCHOOL TITLES • SCIENCE/
RELIGION • SELF-HELP/PSYCHOLOGY
• SPIRITUAL SEARCH • WORLD
RELIGIONS/SCRIPTURES • YOGA

Please visit our website,
**www.O-books.net**